Organising and Planning Guide

Heinemann Educational Publishers
Halley Court, Jordan Hill, Oxford, OX2 8EJ
a division of Harcourt Education Ltd

Heinemann is a registered trademark of Harcourt Education Ltd

Writing team

John T Blair

Percy W Farren

Myra A Pearson

John W Thayers

David K Thomson

First published 2003

08 07 06 05 04 03
10 9 8 7 6 5 4 3 2 1

ISBN 0435 17981 0

Designed and illustrated by Bridge Creative Services Limited, Bicester, Oxon.
Printed and bound in Great Britain by Ashford Colour Press, Gosport, Hants.

Acknowledgements
The outcomes and targets listed in the charts on pages 30–43 and 51–52 are from
Mathematics 5–14 © The Scottish Office Education Department.

Contents

1 Introducing Scottish Heinemann Maths

Mathematical development

Scottish Heinemann Maths is a course designed to help teachers implement the teaching approaches described in Improving Mathematics Education 5–14. Its clearly defined structure provides progression from Primary 1 to Primary 7 and offers schools a teaching programme with both coherence and continuity.

There is an emphasis on direct, interactive teaching aimed at helping children to develop a range of mental calculation strategies. These include the ability to recall basic facts quickly, calculate accurately with pencil and paper, use appropriate mathematical vocabulary and make connections between different areas of mathematics.

Effective teaching

Each mathematical topic in the *Teaching File* is developed systematically through a series of carefully structured lessons and linked *Pupil Activities*. The lessons provide the opportunity for direct, interactive teaching, and oral and mental work involving groups or the whole class on a daily basis.

Pupil Activities are provided to consolidate key teaching ideas and support group work, differentiation and discussion. Some of the small group activities require the children to work together in order to play a game or solve a problem. Suggestions on a range of simple and effective teaching resources to help motivate the children, illustrate a key teaching approach or enhance participation are included for each topic in the *Teaching File*.

Classroom organisation

The components of **Scottish Heinemann Maths** are designed for use in a flexible way. This ensures that the needs of children and teacher are met, whatever form of classroom organisation is used. Interactive *Teaching* activities can be used with a large group or a whole class. There are suitably differentiated *Pupil Activities* and written practice, consolidation, application and extension work in the *Textbook* and *Extension Textbook* designed for use with groups, individuals or the whole class. These can be used to allow the teacher to work uninterrupted with any children needing additional support.

Mental calculation

The course stresses the importance of children developing the ability to 'work things out in their heads'. There is, therefore, an emphasis on oral, mental mathematics, rapid random recall of basic number facts and children explaining their methods. To acquire the necessary skills and the confidence to do this, number facts and a range of mental calculation strategies are taught and practised in a systematic way. Children are encouraged to memorise these facts and to use mental strategies when they cannot recall them.

Planning for learning

Detailed advice and examples of long- and short-term plans are given on pages 17–20 of this *Organising and Planning Guide*. The emphasis is on creating a coherent and manageable form of planning that reflects the guidance given in Improving Mathematics Education 5–14.

Assessment and recording

Scottish Heinemann Maths provides a range of assessment materials designed to help the teacher build up a detailed picture of the children's attainment and to check that attainment targets are being met. These materials complement the teacher's ongoing informal assessments, which are carried out on a daily basis by interacting with children or observing them at work.

The assessment material may cover a short section of work in a *Check-up*, or a whole topic in a *Topic Assessment*, or provide an end-of-year *Round-up* where different areas of mathematics are assessed. The materials can be used as part of the process of giving feedback to children and to remind them of the progress they have made. They also provide a comprehensive record of achievement that can be shared with parents and other teachers.

Involving parents

Home Activities can be used to support a school's commitment of actively involving parents in their child's learning. They provide a number of straightforward activities that give parents confidence in helping their child with mathematics. For the child, *Home Activities* provide opportunities for further practice and consolidation.

Scottish Heinemann Maths components

SHM 6 consists of the following components.

For teachers: *Organising and Planning Guide*
Teaching File
Teaching Resource Book
Answer Book

For children: *Textbook*
Extension Textbook
Assessment Booklet (including *Check-ups, Topic Assessments* and a *Round-up* test)
Pupil Sheets (included in the *Teaching Resource Book*)
Home Activities (included in the *Teaching Resource Book*)
Resource Sheets (included in the *Teaching Resource Book*).

Organising and Planning Guide

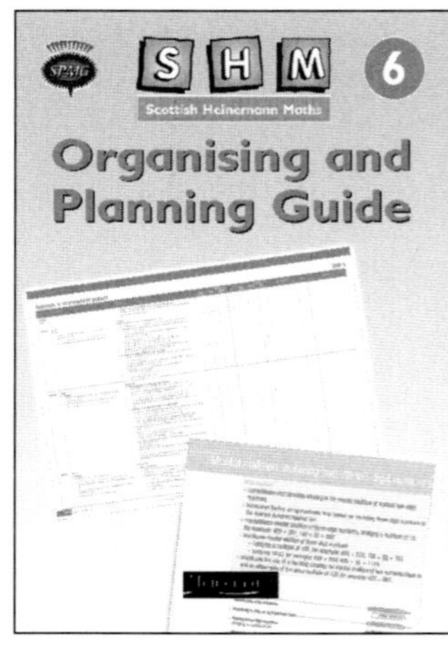

- The guide outlines:
  - the main features of the course
  - the component parts of **SHM 6**.
- It provides advice about:
  - planning to use the course effectively
  - organising resources
  - teaching lessons and follow-up work
  - assessing learning.
- Also included are:
  - charts to show the mathematical content of **SHM 5** and **SHM 6**.
  - a mapping to the Level D attainment targets in a development planner for the year
  - an example of a weekly planner
  - pupil record charts
  - an assessment record grid
  - a Level D class record grid.

Teaching File

- The file contains:
  - a bank of *Starters and other mental activities* to supplement those included in lessons throughout the file
  - teaching notes giving suggestions for lessons, pupil activities, further teaching, the use of the *Textbook* and *Extension Textbook* pages, follow-up activities and assessment
  - references to photocopiable *Pupil Sheets* for use either within a lesson or as follow-up practice, consolidation or extension
  - references to photocopiable *Home Activities* to give homework linked to the work in school.

Starters and other mental activities

- The *Teaching File* has a bank of suggestions for oral mental activities. These are intended to promote a 'feel' for number, quick recall of number facts and the flexible use of mental calculation strategies. They are designed to be interactive, involving the teacher and a large group or the whole class.

Used as 'starters' at the beginning of lessons, the activities help to keep skills 'ticking over', even when the main teaching has moved to another topic. They can, however, be used at any time for practice or consolidation, as well as to check whether children are ready for the next step.

- Some of the activities are *generic*, providing a 'format' which can be adapted to suit different topics. The remainder are linked to *specific* topics. This activity relates to 'Numbers to millions'.

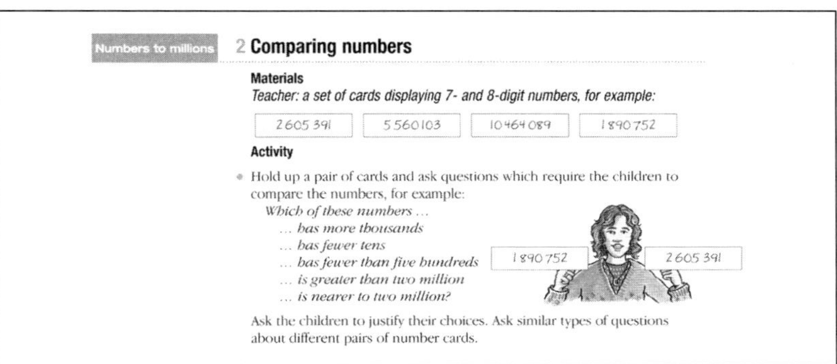

Teaching notes

- **SHM 6** includes the following mathematical topics:

Numbers to millions	Fractions	Volume/Capacity
Addition	Decimals	Area
Subtraction	Percentages	2D Shape
Multiplication	Time	3D Shape
Division	Length	Position, Movement and Angle
Number Properties	Weight	Data Handling

- At the beginning of each topic a summary page provides:
  - a description of related *Previous work*
  - a concise *Overview* of the work of the new topic
  - a *Development* section, which details the mathematical content and suggested teaching approaches for the topic

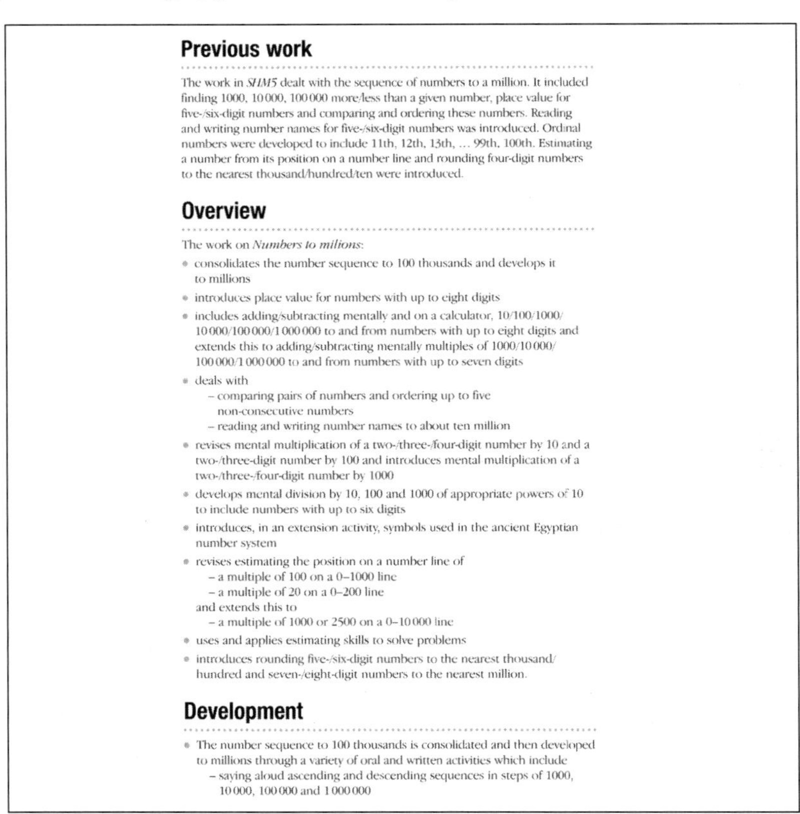

– a *Contents* table containing references to teacher and pupil materials
required for each section within the topic

– a *Language* list of relevant mathematical vocabulary

– a *Resources* list, which outlines general materials and specific *Resource Sheets*.

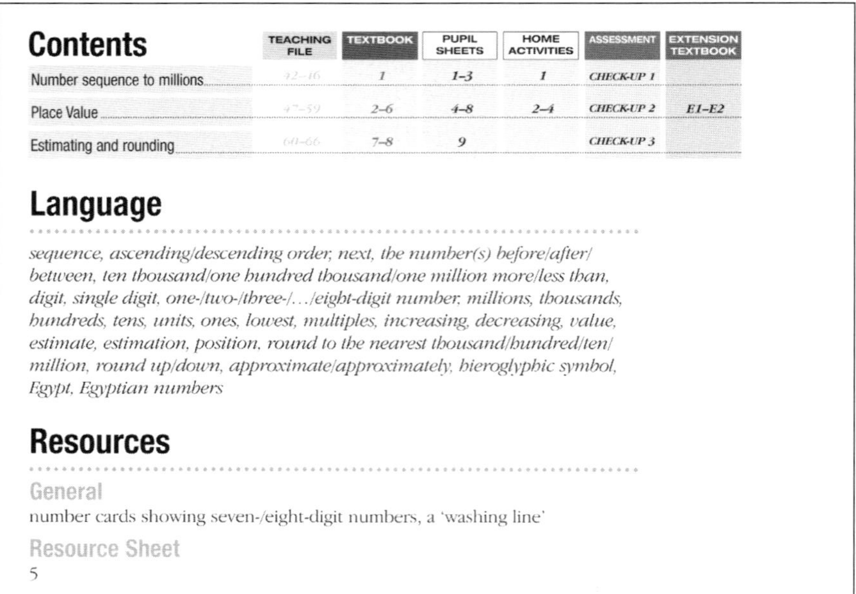

- The notes for each section within a topic follow the same pattern.

  A brief statement outlines the work covered by the section.

  A *Schematic* diagram details the lessons within the section. It shows how all
  the associated materials in **SHM 6** fit together and progress through the work
  of the section.

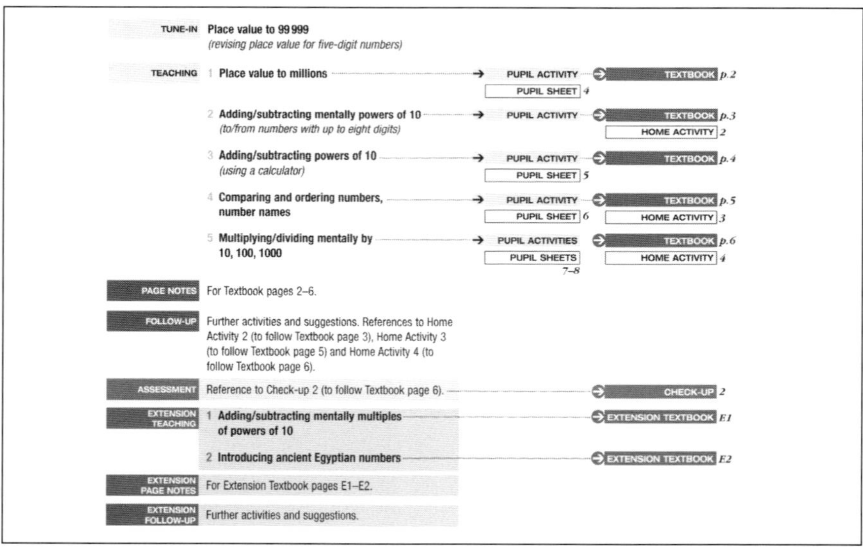

A *Tune-in* is then provided as a suggestion for starting the teaching. This is an interactive, mental, whole class activity which revises any relevant previous work and sets the scene for the first lesson of the section.

An activity from the bank of *Starters and other mental activities* can be used, if required, as a lead-in to a subsequent lesson. Alternatively, an activity from the previous day's work can be adapted for this purpose.

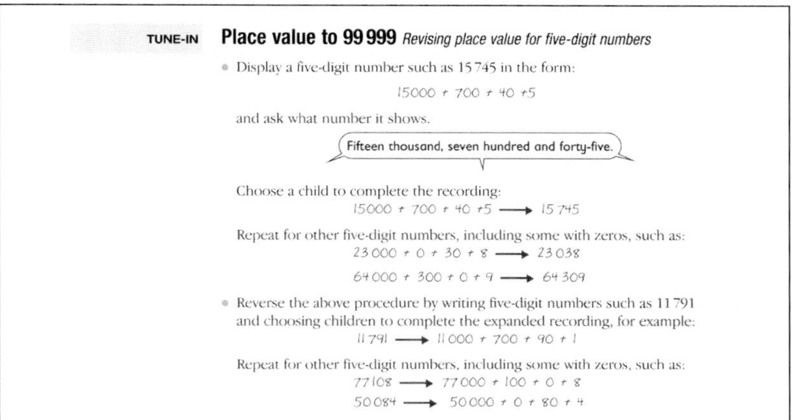

Teaching suggestions are given for group or class lessons to develop the sequence of work in the section.

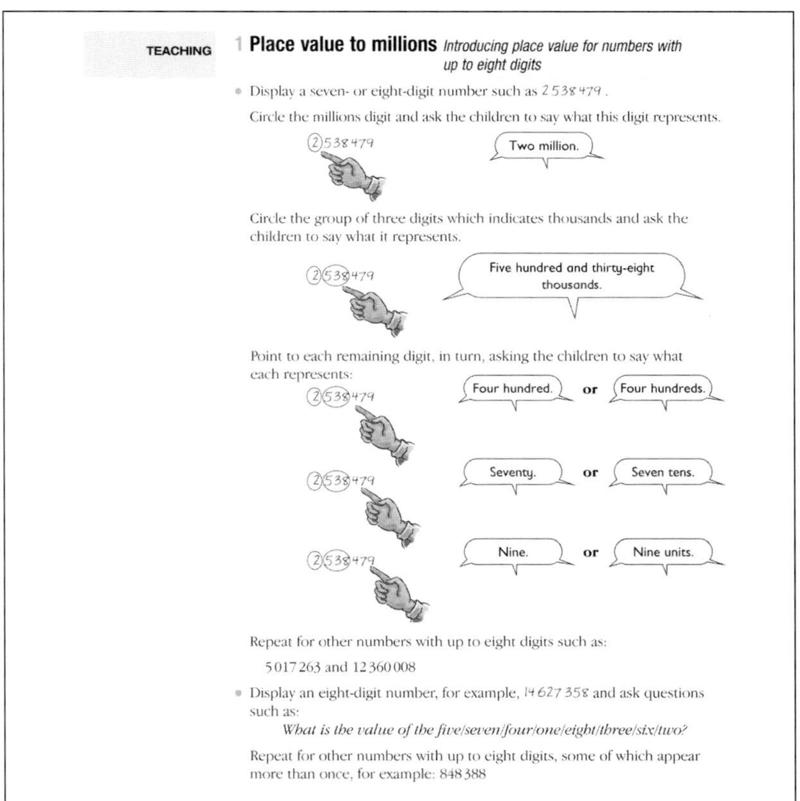

Pupil Activities, including practical activities, games and mental work, follow many of the *Teaching* suggestions. These are designed to be used by groups, pairs or individuals, with some teacher support. When several activities are provided, a selection should be made to suit groups within the class.

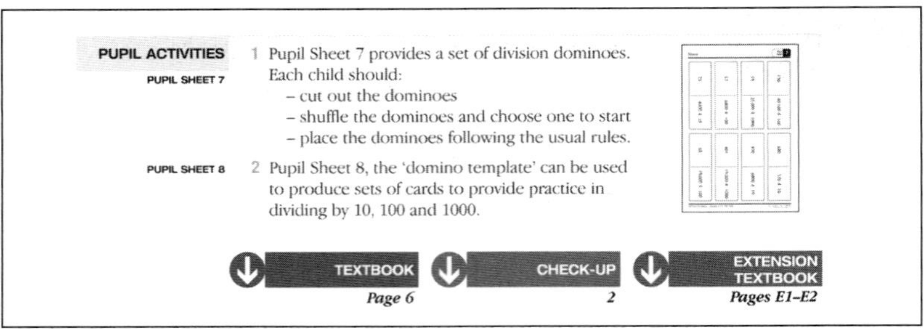

References to *Textbook* pages point to appropriate written work for pupils.

References are given to *Further Teaching*, if any.

Suggestions for *Further Teaching* lessons with the class or a group provide alternative/complementary approaches or further development. The following introduces a specific mental strategy for *Addition*.

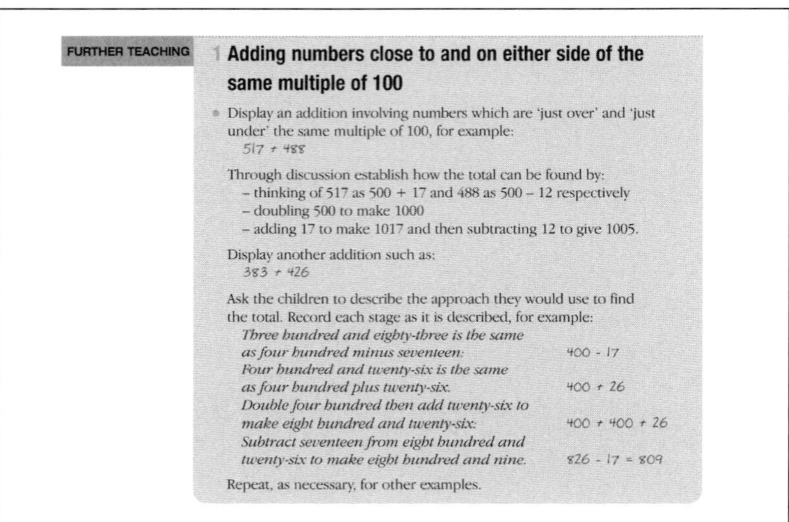

Page Notes offer advice about using the relevant *Textbook* pages. The notes highlight more challenging examples and possible difficulties with language and instructions.

Follow-up suggestions are given for drawing lessons to a close. These often involve discussion, mental work, extension activities or further practice.

References are also given to *Home Activities* related to the *Textbook* pages.

The Assessment section may include:
- a reference to a *Check-up* associated with the work of the section
- page notes for *Topic Assessments*.

The *Topic Assessments* are designed to assess a number, measure, shape or data handling topic in a broad way, covering the work of several sections, or a single section in the case of a short topic. The notes point out some common errors that may occur and make some suggestions for dealing with them. For each question there are references to relevant *Textbook* pages and the appropriate section of the *Teaching File,* should some re-teaching or additional practice be required.

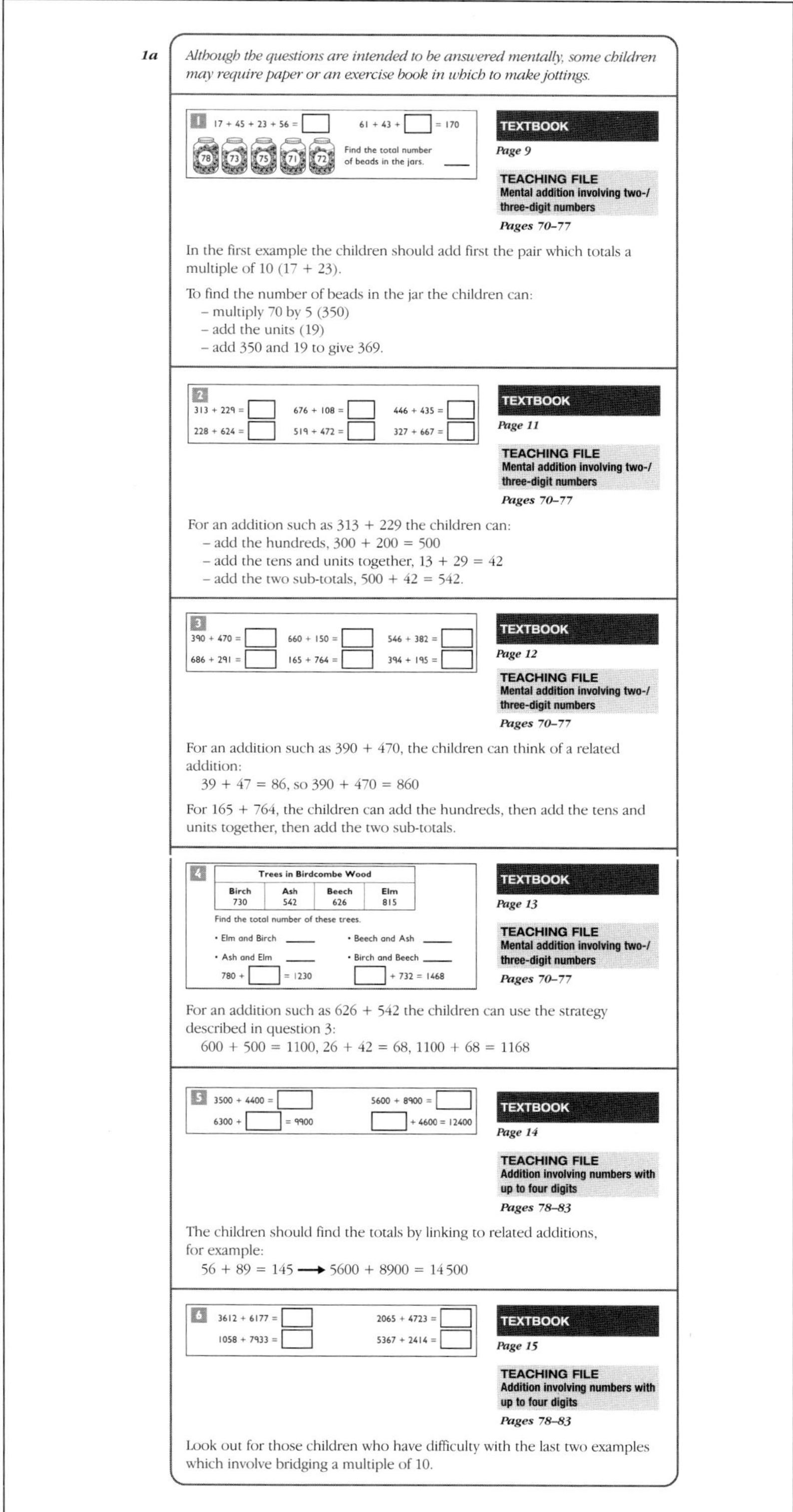

1a *Although the questions are intended to be answered mentally, some children may require paper or an exercise book in which to make jottings.*

1 $17 + 45 + 23 + 56 =$ ☐ $61 + 43 +$ ☐ $= 170$

Find the total number of beads in the jars. ____

TEXTBOOK
Page 9

TEACHING FILE
Mental addition involving two-/three-digit numbers
Pages 70–77

In the first example the children should add first the pair which totals a multiple of 10 (17 + 23).

To find the number of beads in the jar the children can:
- multiply 70 by 5 (350)
- add the units (19)
- add 350 and 19 to give 369.

2 $313 + 229 =$ ☐ $676 + 108 =$ ☐ $446 + 435 =$ ☐
$228 + 624 =$ ☐ $519 + 472 =$ ☐ $327 + 667 =$ ☐

TEXTBOOK
Page 11

TEACHING FILE
Mental addition involving two-/three-digit numbers
Pages 70–77

For an addition such as 313 + 229 the children can:
- add the hundreds, 300 + 200 = 500
- add the tens and units together, 13 + 29 = 42
- add the two sub-totals, 500 + 42 = 542.

3 $390 + 470 =$ ☐ $660 + 150 =$ ☐ $546 + 382 =$ ☐
$686 + 291 =$ ☐ $165 + 764 =$ ☐ $394 + 195 =$ ☐

TEXTBOOK
Page 12

TEACHING FILE
Mental addition involving two-/three-digit numbers
Pages 70–77

For an addition such as 390 + 470, the children can think of a related addition:
39 + 47 = 86, so 390 + 470 = 860

For 165 + 764, the children can add the hundreds, then add the tens and units together, then add the two sub-totals.

4

Trees in Birdcombe Wood			
Birch	Ash	Beech	Elm
730	542	626	815

Find the total number of these trees.

- Elm and Birch ____   • Beech and Ash ____
- Ash and Elm ____   • Birch and Beech ____
- $780 +$ ☐ $= 1230$ ☐ $+ 732 = 1468$

TEXTBOOK
Page 13

TEACHING FILE
Mental addition involving two-/three-digit numbers
Pages 70–77

For an addition such as 626 + 542 the children can use the strategy described in question 3:
600 + 500 = 1100, 26 + 42 = 68, 1100 + 68 = 1168

5 $3500 + 4400 =$ ☐ $5600 + 8900 =$ ☐
$6300 +$ ☐ $= 9900$ ☐ $+ 4600 = 12400$

TEXTBOOK
Page 14

TEACHING FILE
Addition involving numbers with up to four digits
Pages 78–83

The children should find the totals by linking to related additions, for example:
56 + 89 = 145 ⟶ 5600 + 8900 = 14 500

6 $3612 + 6177 =$ ☐ $2065 + 4723 =$ ☐
$1058 + 7933 =$ ☐ $5367 + 2414 =$ ☐

TEXTBOOK
Page 15

TEACHING FILE
Addition involving numbers with up to four digits
Pages 78–83

Look out for those children who have difficulty with the last two examples which involve bridging a multiple of 10.

Teaching Resource Book

- The book contains:
  - photocopiable *Pupil Sheets* for use either within a lesson or as follow-up practice, consolidation or extension
  - photocopiable *Home Activities* to give homework linked to the work in school
  - photocopiable *Resource Sheets* for use by the teacher/children during lessons.

Pupil Sheets

- The **SHM 6** *Teaching Resource Book* includes 58 photocopiable *Pupil Sheets*. There are several types which have different purposes. For example:
  - to provide a means of recording during the course of a lesson
  - to give extra practice to children who have completed the *Textbook* pages but need more examples
  - to provide a template for teachers to produce their own sheets, which can be customised to cater for different ability levels.

Home Activities

- The **SHM 6** *Teaching Resource Book* contains 23 *Home Activities* and 3 *Home Sheets* of associated 'cards' for use with some of them. These are photocopiable.

  The activities aim to:
  - provide important extra practice for the child
  - give parents an opportunity to be actively involved with their child's learning and provide encouragement and help
  - inform those at home about the mathematics being taught in school.

- *Home Activities* are referenced from:
  - the foot of the *Textbook* page which completes this work in school
  - the *Follow-up* section in the *Teaching File* for the related *Textbook* page.

- There are two types of *Home Activity*:

  - simple oral, mental activities or games involving an adult and the child. There are straight-forward instructions for the adult which give examples of the language to be used
  - written practice examples for the child to complete and the adult to check.

  Often both types appear on one sheet. However, it is not necessary to use both parts at the same time.

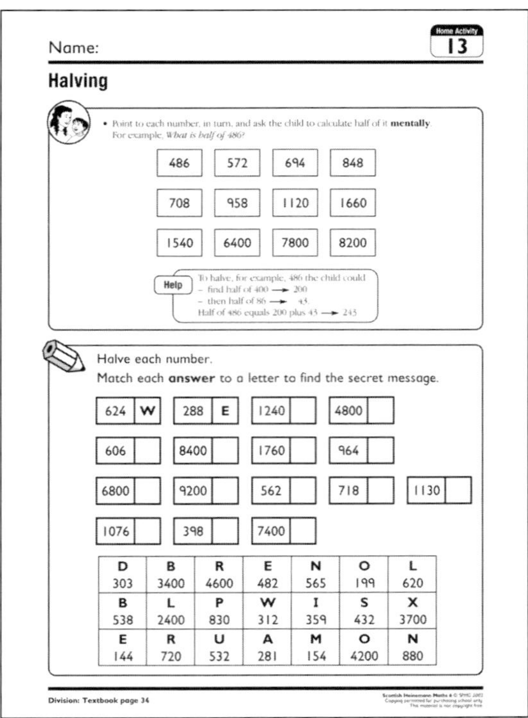

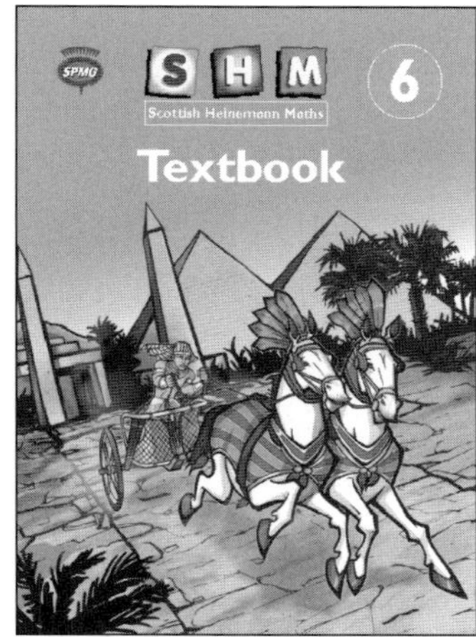

Resource Sheets

- The **SHM6** *Teaching Resource Book* includes 46 photocopiable *Resource Sheets* for producing materials such as flashcards, number cards, 100-squares and so on, for use when teaching lessons.

Textbook

- The *Textbook* contains written work for the children for use after the *Teaching* of a lesson and related *Pupil Activities* have been completed. The pages provide practice, consolidation and application.

This page follows the *Teaching* about mental division beyond the tables in the 'Division' section.

- There are references at the foot of some of the *Textbook* pages to:
    - *Check-ups*, which assess the work of a section
    - *Home Activities*, which provide related work for a child and adult at home
    - *Topic Assessments*, which assess in a broad way the work related to a number, measure, shape or data handling topic.

Extension Textbook

- The *Extension Textbook* includes a range of activities to provide both lateral and vertical extension. Throughout the book children are encouraged to use and apply their knowledge and skills through problem solving and enquiry.

The page shown overleaf follows the core work on *Data Handling*.

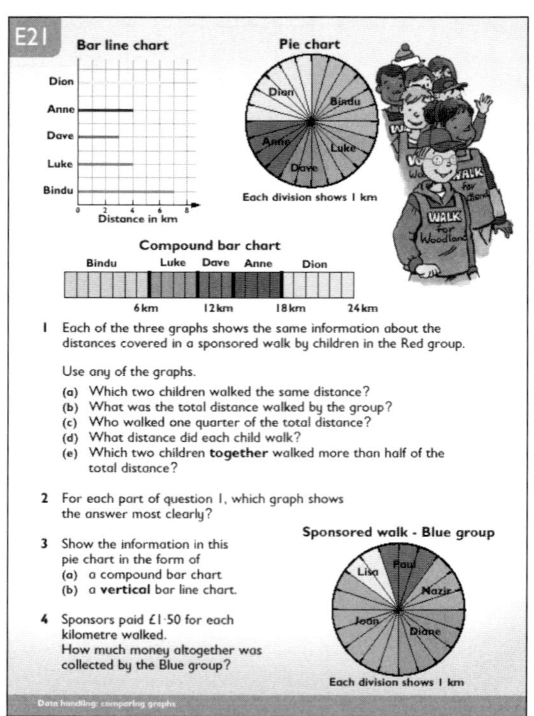

Assessment Book

- The *Assessment* book includes:
  - *Check-ups*
  - *Topic Assessments*
  - a *Round-up.*

- It is designed to assess children's understanding, knowledge and ability to apply skills and techniques. The assessments are provided in both booklet and photocopy master format. The **SHM 6** *Assessment* book contains:
  - 19 *Check-ups* covering the topics shown:

Numbers to millions	– 3	Division	– 2
Addition	– 2	Fractions	– 2
Subtraction	– 2	Decimals	– 6
Multiplication	– 2		

  - 15 *Topic Assessments* covering:

Addition	Number properties	Time	2D shape
Subtraction	Fractions	Length	Position, movement
Multiplication	Decimals	Weight	and Angle
Division	Percentages	Area	Data Handling

  - 1 Level D *Round-up* test containing questions on number, money, shape, measure and data handling.

- Each *Check-up* covers a smaller range of work within a single topic and is linked to the work of several *Textbook* pages. One of the *Check-ups* for *Multiplication* is shown here:

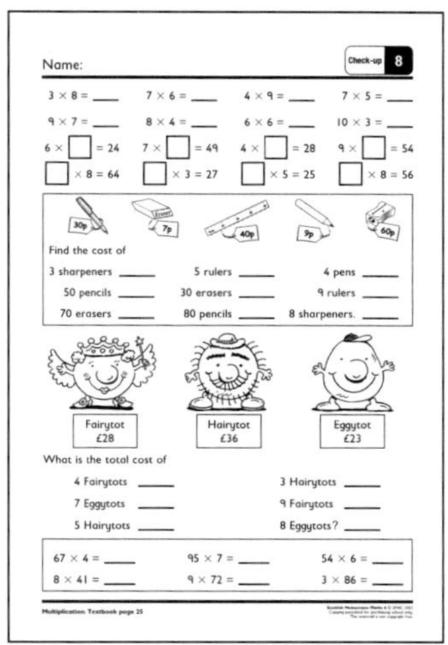

References to *Check-ups* are given in the *Teaching File* and at the foot of appropriate *Textbook* pages.

- The *Topic Assessments* cover work related to a whole topic. References to *Topic Assessments* are given in the *Teaching File*, at the end of the appropriate section of notes, and at the foot of the appropriate *Textbook* pages.

- The Level D *Round-up* covers a wide range of 'mixed' mathematics and gives an indication of overall level of attainment.

Answer Book

- The *Answer Book* contains answers for the:
    - *Textbook*
    - *Extension Textbook*
    - *Pupil Sheets*
    - *Assessment*
    - *Home Activities*.

3 Using Scottish Heinemann Maths

Learning and teaching

The approach to learning and teaching in **SHM 6** is based on the following key ideas:
- daily mathematics lessons
- direct, interactive teaching
- systematic development of mental and written methods of calculation.

Given this approach, the *Teaching File* is a crucial component of **SHM 6**, as it provides guidance on:
- the development of each mathematical topic in a clear, systematic way
- teaching, pupil activities and follow-up work to promote understanding and develop and apply skills
- the effective use of resources to develop knowledge and understanding of key aspects of number work
- the use of mental and oral activities to develop and practise mental strategies and techniques.

Direct teaching is essential. It cannot be replaced by the use of *Pupil Sheets*, *Textbook* and other course materials. The function of such materials is to:
- check the children's understanding of what has been taught
- provide a record of work completed
- set new challenges where the children can apply the mathematics they have learned.

The **SHM 6** pupil materials are **not** designed to teach new concepts to children working through them on their own, without prior teaching and discussion. The focus is very much on direct teaching and interaction.

Direct teaching and interaction

High quality direct teaching and interaction are at the heart of **Scottish Heinemann Maths**. This two-way process encourages both teachers and children to be actively engaged in the learning process.

Children are expected to:
- be actively involved in answering questions
- contribute to discussion during *Teaching* activities and *Follow-up* discussions
- be able to explain and demonstrate understanding of their learning to others.

The *Teaching File* makes suggestions which enable the teacher to provide an effective direct teaching approach through an appropriate balance of the following methods.

Demonstration – showing and illustrating mathematics using appropriate resources and visual materials.

Teaching File, page 184
Fractions

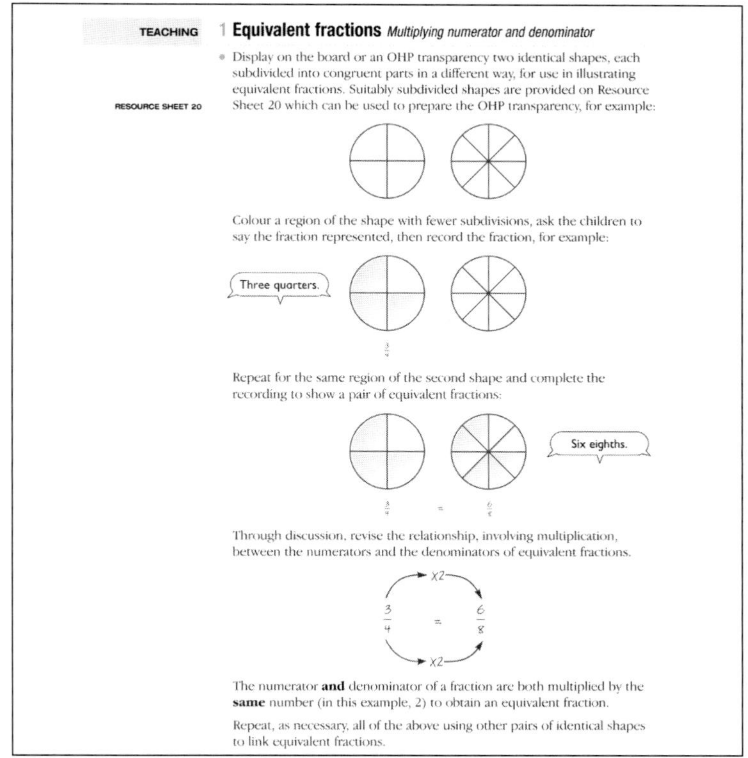

Instruction – giving information clearly and precisely.

Teaching File, page 222
Decimals

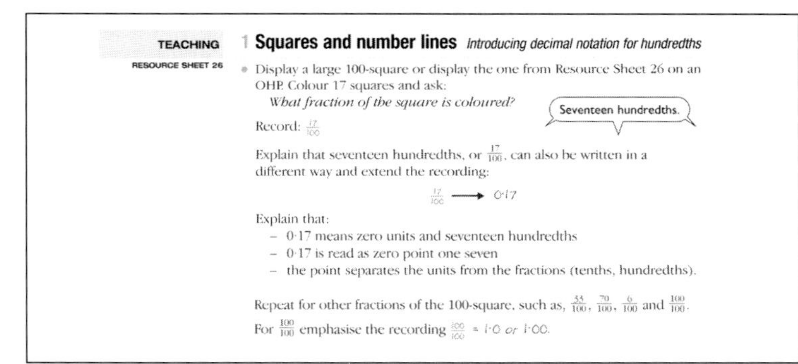

Direction – sharing teaching objectives with the children and making sure they know what they should be learning.

Teaching File, page 352
Position, movement and angle

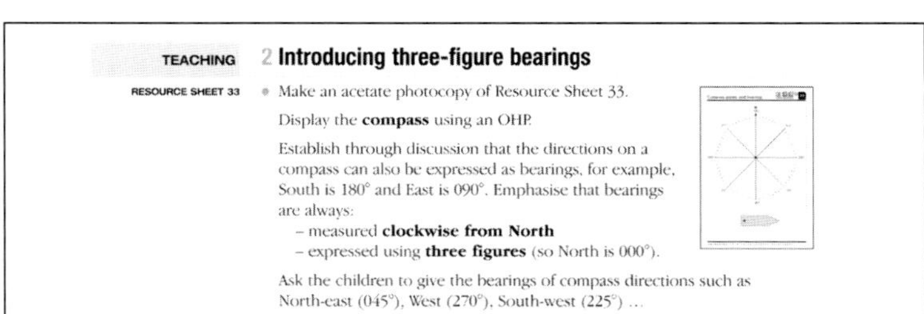

Explanation and illustration – giving accurate, well-paced explanations.

Teaching File, page 168
Number Properties

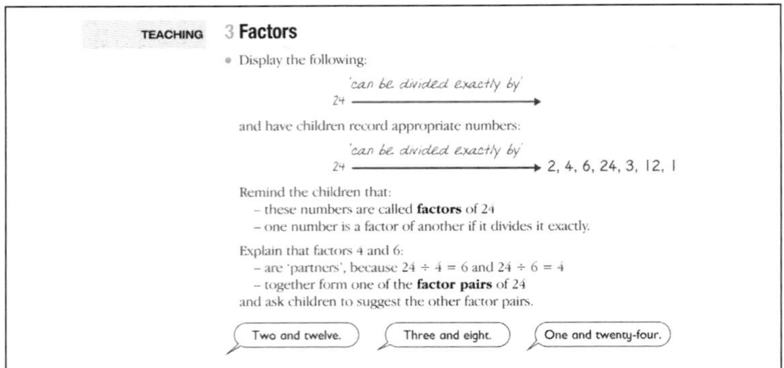

Questioning – using effective questioning techniques to:
- ensure that children are actively involved in their learning
- encourage the children to explain what they are doing
- help the children to consider other possible strategies and methods
- focus the children's attention on new aspects of their learning.

A wide range of open and closed questions is suggested within the *Teaching* activities in **SHM 6**.

Consolidating – maximising opportunities to reinforce and develop what has been taught through the use of:
- *Starters and other mental activities* to consolidate previous learning
- well-focused *Pupil Activities* and *Pupil Sheets*
- practice and applications in the *Textbook*
- extension activities in the *Extension Textbook*.

Discussion and evaluation of children's responses – identifying mistakes and misunderstandings by using:
- oral *Follow-up* activities from the *Teaching File*
- *Check-ups* and *Topic Assessments* in the *Assessment* book.

This process can help to identify appropriate further teaching.

Summarising – reviewing with the children what has been taught and what the children have learned using:
- *Follow-up* activities.

Differentiation

Scottish Heinemann Maths has been designed to be used with the whole class, groups of children or individual children. The *Teaching* activities in the *Teaching File* have been written for group or whole class teaching, but can be adapted for use with individuals.

The following features of **SHM 6** can help the teacher to plan differentiated programmes:

- the ability to select from the suggested *Teaching* activities and *Pupil Activities* for each section in the *Teaching File* allows the teacher to plan appropriate programmes to match the children's needs
- *Pupil Sheets* provide further practice for those who need it. Some of them provide templates for teachers to customise for use with groups or individuals
- the activities within the *Extension Textbook* provide both lateral and vertical extension. They provide opportunities to extend children's thinking and learning.

The teacher should omit pages, parts of pages or questions in the *Textbook* which are not appropriate for specific children. However, all children should have experience of using and applying the mathematics they are learning.

Planning

Starting points

Planning for effective learning involves thinking about:

- the advice contained in Improving Mathematics Education 5–14 and in the Mathematics 5–14 Guidelines.
  The chart on pages 28–41 summarises the curriculum coverage provided by **SHM 6**.

- the children's previous experience in mathematics.
  This can be found by consulting:
  - the children's records of achievement
  - the mathematical development chart on pages 46–47.

- the development of the children's knowledge, skills and understanding.

Information relating to the work contained in **SHM 6** is found in:
- the pupil record grids on pages 53–55 of this guide
- the summary at the beginning of each new topic in the *Teaching File*. It describes *Previous work* and gives an *Overview* and a detailed *Development* of the topic. The *Contents* table lists the sections within the topic and all the **SHM 6** materials associated with them. The *Language* list gives a clear indication of the vocabulary used.

While there are many ways to plan a mathematics programme and schools will have their own planning formats, **SHM 6** provides examples of a development planner, a block planner and a weekly planner. These are designed to provide a route through the materials.

Development planner

The development planner illustrates a progression in the teaching of each maths topic in **SHM 6**. The content of **SHM 6** has been divided into a number of planning units.

Detailed planners are included on pages 30–43 of this guide.

Appendix A: Development planner — SHM 6

SHM Resources columns: Teaching File page, Textbook, Extension Textbook, Pupil Sheet, Home Activity. Assessment columns: Check-up, Topic Assessment.

Unit	Mathematics 5–14	SHM Topic	Teaching File page	Textbook	Extension Textbook	Pupil Sheet	Home Activity	Check-up	Topic Assessment	Other resources	Date	Comment
Number 1 (cont.)		– includes problem solving activities which involve estimating quantities – introduces rounding a five-/six-digit number to the nearest 1000/100 and a seven-/eight-digit number to the nearest million.										
Number 2	AS/D • Add: – mentally for 2 digit whole numbers, beyond in some cases, involving multiples of 10 or 100 – without a calculator, for 4 digits with at most two decimal places – with a calculator, for 4 digits with at most two decimal places.	Addition • Mental addition involving two-/three-digit numbers – consolidates and develops strategies for mental addition of several two-digit numbers – introduces finding an approximate total based on rounding three-digit numbers to the nearest hundred/nearest ten – consolidates mental addition of three-digit numbers, bridging a multiple of 10, for example: 428 + 267, 149 + ■ = 682 – introduces mental addition of three-digit numbers – bridging a multiple of 100, for example: 493 + 272, 193 + ■ = 753 – bridging 1000, for example: 635 + 853, 650 + ■ = 1170 – introduces the use of a doubling strategy for mental addition of two numbers close to and on either side of the same multiple of 100, for example: 421 + 387.	70–77	9–13		10	5	4				
		• Addition involving numbers with up to four digits – introduces mental addition of four-digit multiples of 100, for example: 6100 + 2300, 4400 + 3800, 6500 + 7600 – introduces mental addition of four-digit numbers with no bridging (2634 + 2352) then bridging a multiple of 10 only (4564 + 2107) – further develops the use of a standard written method of addition of: – two numbers with four digits – several numbers with different numbers of digits to include totals greater than 10 000.	78–83	14–18			6	5	1a, b			
Number 3	AS/D • Subtract: – mentally for 2 digit whole numbers, beyond in some cases, involving multiples of 10 or 100 – without a calculator, for 4 digits with at most two decimal places – with a calculator, for 4 digits with at most two decimal places.	Subtraction • Mental subtraction involving three-digit numbers – revises mental subtraction of a two-digit number from a three-digit number – revises mental subtraction involving three-digit multiples of 10 (550 – 260) and introduces mental subtraction, bridging a multiple of 100: – of a three-digit multiple of 10 from any three-digit number (768 – 380) – of any three-digit number from a three-digit multiple of 10 (650 – 464) – introduces mental subtraction of three-digit numbers, bridging a multiple of 10 (862 – 349).	90–95	19–21			7	6				
		• Subtraction involving numbers with four or more digits – revises mental subtraction from a four-digit multiple of 100 and then from any four-digit number of a three-digit multiple of 100 (4300 – 600 8197 – 500) – introduces mental subtraction from a four-digit multiple of 100 of – another four-digit multiple of 100, bridging a multiple of 1000 (7300 – 6800) – a four-digit multiple of 50, not bridging a multiple of 1000 (8400 - 5150) – introduces mental subtraction from a multiple of 1000 of any three-/four-digit number (2000 – 754, 8000 – 2785) – introduces mental subtraction from a four-digit number of a three-/four-digit number – with no bridging (3956 – 703, 7568 – 1352) – bridging a multiple of 10 only (2894 – 745, 6722 – 2607) – consolidates a standard written method of subtraction and includes subtractions involving four-digit numbers …	96–103	22–24	3	11–12	8	7	2a, b			

Block planner

The block planner indentifies one possible way of organising the content of **SHM 6** over the course of a year. The year is divided into six, 6 week teaching blocks.

Detailed planners are included on pages 44–47 of this guide.

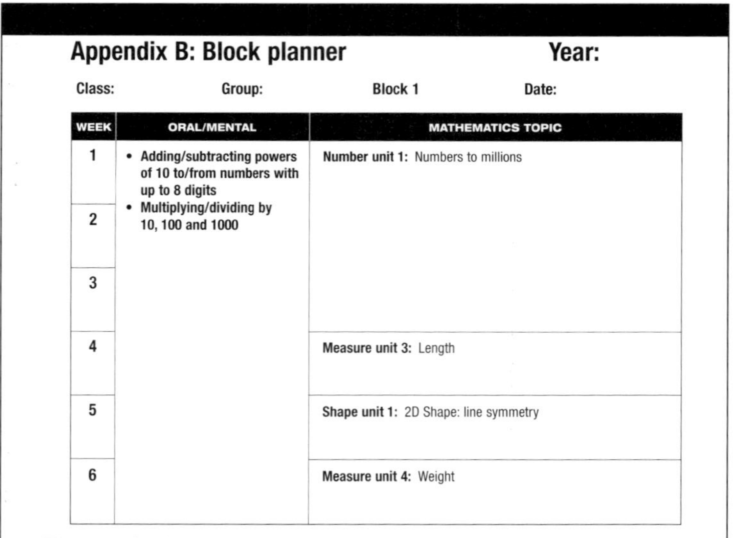

Appendix B: Block planner — Year:

Class:　　　Group:　　　Block 1　　　Date:

WEEK	ORAL/MENTAL	MATHEMATICS TOPIC
1	• Adding/subtracting powers of 10 to/from numbers with up to 8 digits	Number unit 1: Numbers to millions
2	• Multiplying/dividing by 10, 100 and 1000	
3		
4		Measure unit 3: Length
5		Shape unit 1: 2D Shape: line symmetry
6		Measure unit 4: Weight

Weekly planner

It is often necessary to plan in more detail on a weekly or daily basis. Plans of this type provide an indication of what the teacher hopes to cover during the course of the week. However, given that the mathematics must necessarily build on the needs of the children, an element of flexibility should be built in. This allows for modification to the plan as it is implemented.

The *Schematic* diagrams at the beginning of each section in the *Teaching File* provide a helpful starting point for this process.

Teaching File, page 112
Multiplication

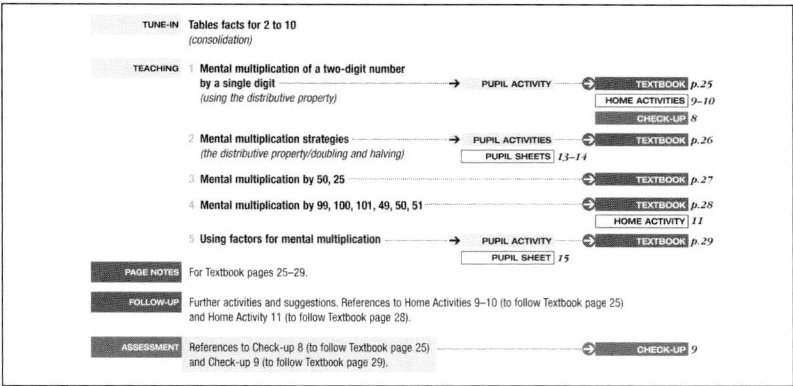

The weekly planner on page 22 shows how *Mental multiplication* might be developed over the course of a week.

SECTION	Monday	Tuesday	Wednesday	Thursday	Friday
	Mental multiplication				
TUNE-IN or STARTER	**Tune-in** **Table facts for 2 to 10** (consolidation) *T.F. 113*	Activity from *Starters and other mental activities* related to multiplying a two-digit number by a single digit	Activity from *Starters and other mental activities* related to multiplying using doubling/halving	Activity from *Starters and other mental activities* highlighting halving/distributive property strategies	Activity from *Starters and other mental activities* related to multiplying by 99, 100, 101, 49, 50, 51
TEACHING	1 **Mental multiplication of a two-digit number by a single digit** (using the distributive property) *T.F. 113–114*	2 **Mental multiplication strategies** (the distributive property/doubling and halving) *T.F. 114–117*	3 **Multiplying by 50, 25** *T.F. 117–118*	4 **Mental multiplication by 99, 100, 101, 49, 50, 51** *T.F. 118–119*	5 **Using factors for mental multiplication** *T.F. 119–120*
PUPIL ACTIVITIES	**Pupil activity:** 1 Mental multiplication **Textbook page 25**	**Pupil activities:** **1 Pupil Sheet 13** **2 Pupil Sheet 14** **Textbook page 26**	**Textbook page 27**	**Textbook page 28**	**Pupil activity:** **1 Pupil Sheet 15** **Textbook page 29**
FOLLOW-UP	For **Textbook page 25** **Home activity 9** **Home activity 10**	For **Textbook page 26** **Check-up 8**	For **Textbook page 27**	For **Textbook page 28** **Home activity 11**	For **Textbook page 29** **Check-up 9**
REVIEW	*This would include:* *– key areas of concern to build into the next day's teaching* *– any organisation issues to be addressed* *– any child needing particular help.*				

4 Organising and using the materials

- In the summary at the beginning of each new topic in the *Teaching File* there is a list of *Resources* required for the topic.

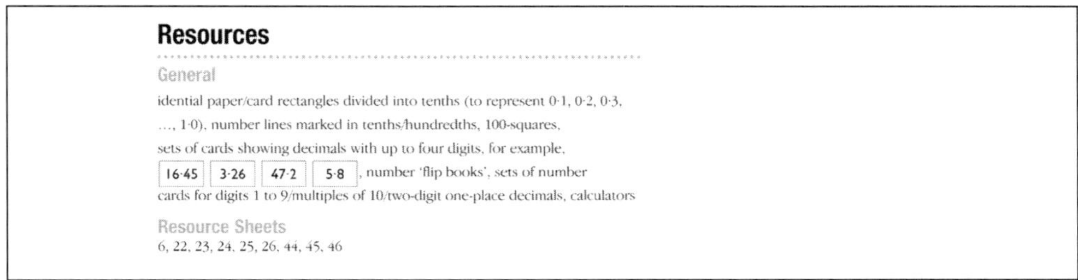

These are listed under two headings – *General* and *Resource Sheets*.

The *General* resources list the types of practical materials that are normally to be found in Primary 6 classrooms. These resources should be easily accessible to the children.

The photocopiable *Resource Sheets* that teachers may wish to use in this section of teaching are indicated. These materials are designed to be used with/by the children.

Other resources such as the necessary *Pupil Sheets*, *Check-ups*, *Topic Assessments*, *Extension* and *Home Activities* are listed in the *Contents* table for the topic and the schematic diagrams for each section.

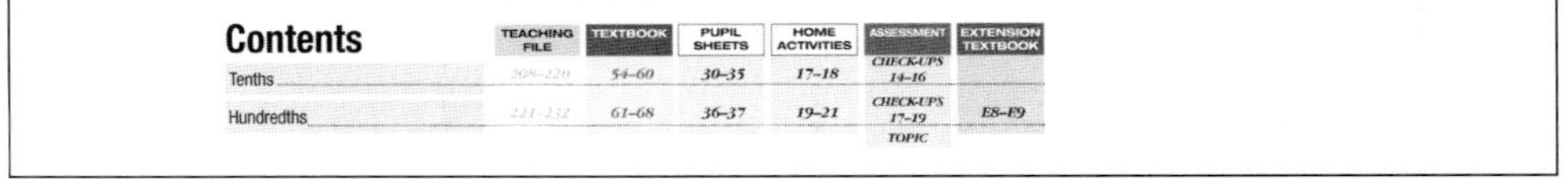

Contents	TEACHING FILE	TEXTBOOK	PUPIL SHEETS	HOME ACTIVITIES	ASSESSMENT	EXTENSION TEXTBOOK
Tenths	208–220	54–60	30–35	17–18	CHECK-UPS 14–16	
Hundredths	221–232	61–68	36–37	19–21	CHECK-UPS 17–19 TOPIC	E8–E9

Teaching File, page 208
Decimals

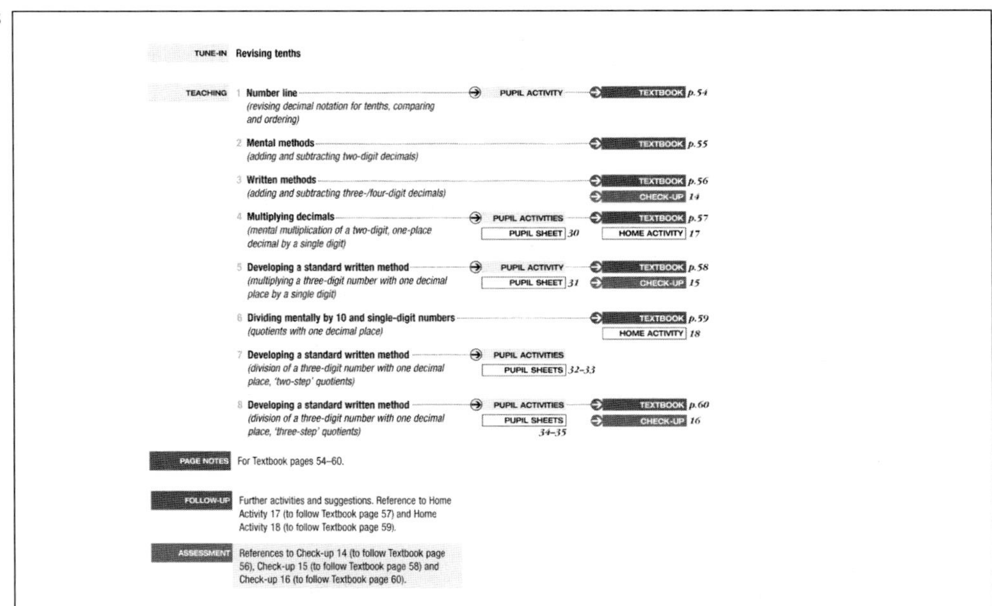

- The materials in **Scottish Heinemann Maths** allow the teacher to structure each mathematics lesson appropriately, for example:
  - **Tune-in** (oral and mental work) using the appropriate *Tune-in*, or an activity from the *Starters and other mental activities* section of the *Teaching File*
  - **Teach/Try** (teaching and practice activities) using *Teaching* and *Pupil Activities*, *Pupil Sheets* and appropriate pages of the *Textbook*, or *Extension Textbook*, described and illustrated in the *Teaching File*
  - **Talkabout** (a follow-up discussion) using further activities and suggestions, for example, from the *Follow-up* to *Textbook* or *Extension Textbook* pages as suggested in the *Teaching File*. The *Follow-up* section also indicates appropriate *Home Activities*.

  The teaching suggestions given in the *Teaching File* do not indicate approximate timings for each part of the lesson. Professional judgement must be used to determine the most appropriate pacing, organisation and specific activities to best meet the needs of the children and the topic. Some flexibility is needed to take account of the children's learning.

- The *Tune-in*, *Teaching* and *Pupil Activities* should be completed before the children attempt related *Textbook* or *Extension Textbook* pages.

  When the children are ready to attempt the *Textbook* page it may be necessary for the teacher to discuss some of the following:
  - what the children have to do, focusing on any concerns with language or the interpretation of instructions
  - where to find any materials they may need
  - how they should set out work or record answers
  - which questions they should complete or omit.

  Teachers, on occasion, may want to ask the children to:
  - do the examples on a *Textbook* page orally without keeping a written record
  - interpret an example in their own words
  - work in pairs or small groups with only one child recording the answers.

  Sometimes it may be appropriate to tackle a page as a discussion with each child writing answers as they go along.

- The follow-up discussion is an important part of the lesson. During this time the teacher may wish to:
  - ask children to show and explain their work to other children
  - draw together what has been learned and, on occasion, extend the work through oral discussion
  - provide tasks for the children to complete at home to consolidate their work in class using, for example, a *Home Activity*
  - make connections to other areas of the curriculum that the children will encounter during the day.

5 Assessment

Day-by-day

Much of the assessment of children's learning of mathematics in the primary classroom is of an informal nature and happens on a daily basis. This can be done during many of the activities that children are involved in such as:
- the *Tune-in* or *Starters and other mental activities*
- the main *Teaching* activity
- the *Pupil Activities*, including games, practical activities, *Pupil Sheets* or *Textbook*
- the *Follow-up* discussion highlighting the main teaching ideas.

These provide evidence which the teacher can use to determine the level of a child's understanding of a particular mathematical idea. The evidence is gathered in a number of different ways over a period of time by:
- listening to and talking with the children (posing questions and noting responses)
- observing the children (noting individual strengths and needs)
- correcting the children's written work
- using the children's self-assessment.

However, more focused methods of assessment are also necessary.

Focused assessment

SHM 6 provides:
- *Check-ups* to assess the children's understanding of a section of work they have recently completed
- *Topic Assessments* to assess a mathematical topic
- a Level D *Round-up* to assess the children's understanding of the range of the mathematics they have been involved in during the course of the year.

Check-ups

When the teacher wishes to use a more objective, specific task to check on the children's understanding of a particular section of teaching in mathematics, for example Mental subtraction involving three-digit numbers, one of the *Check-ups*, can be used. These are provided in the *Assessment* book and in photocopiable format.

A *Check-up* will normally be used after a section of work has been completed. The *Schematics* and *Contents* tables in the summary pages indicate which *Check-up* relates to a particular section of work and when it could be used.

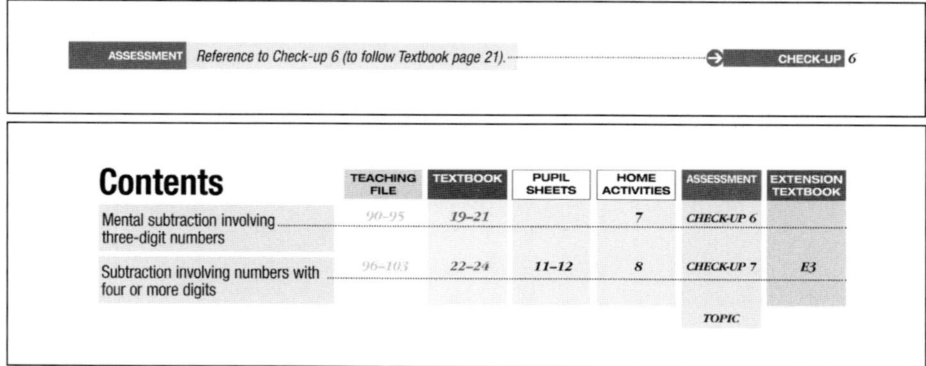

Contents	TEACHING FILE	TEXTBOOK	PUPIL SHEETS	HOME ACTIVITIES	ASSESSMENT	EXTENSION TEXTBOOK
Mental subtraction involving three-digit numbers	90–95	19–21		7	CHECK-UP 6	
Subtraction involving numbers with four or more digits	96–103	22–24	11–12	8	CHECK-UP 7	E3
					TOPIC	

The teaching notes give details of the mathematics covered and the relevant *Textbook* pages for each *Check-up*.

These notes follow the *Page Notes* and suggestions for *Follow-up* activities. The *Check-ups* provide a valuable record of achievement/attainment that can:
- highlight where further teaching and consolidation may be necessary
- be discussed with the child
- be used as a focus of discussion with parents
- be transferred along with other evidence to another teacher or school.

Topic Assessments

The *Assessment* book contains 15 *Topic Assessments*, also available in photocopiable format, which assess the work related to a specific mathematical topic, such as *Subtraction*:

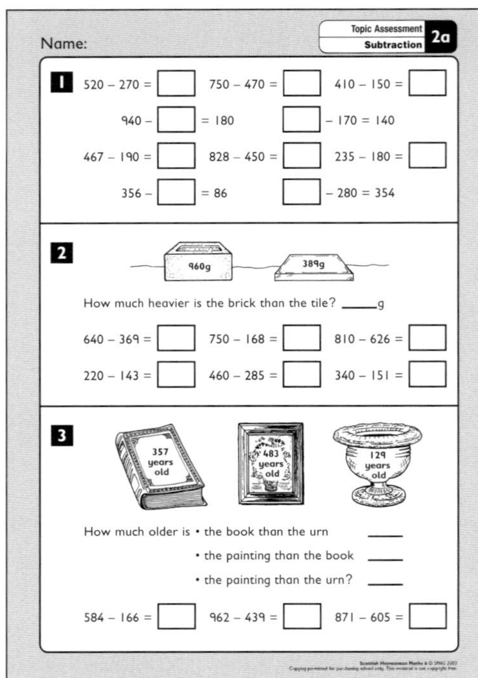

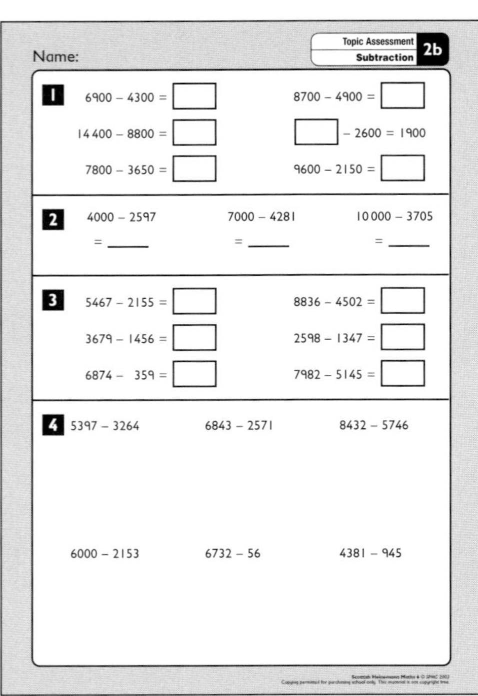

These pages are easily identified by the solid orange border around the whole page. This type of assessment is normally used when a whole topic has been completed.

The *Schematic* diagram at the start of each section indicates where these assessments occur and when they could be used.

The teaching notes give details of:
- the mathematics covered and the relevant *Textbook* pages

- specific equipment or materials required

– what each question is assessing and any common errors children may make
– brief suggestions about how to deal with some repeated errors
– references to the appropriate section of the *Teaching File* to return to if further teaching or consolidation is required.

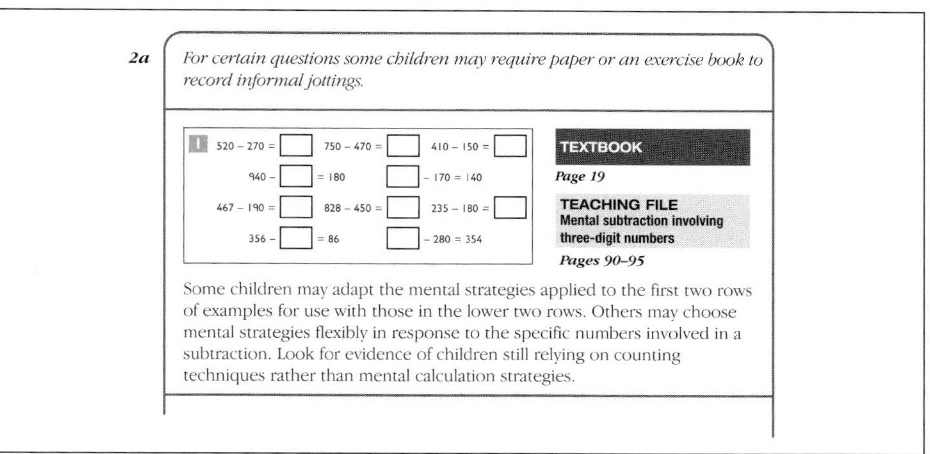

Round-up assessments

The end-of-year *Round-up* assessment checks on the full range of the mathematics covered.

The *Round-up* is provided in the *Assessment* book and is also available in photocopiable format.

Completion of the *Round-up* provides evidence of how well the children are progressing towards the attainment targets for Level D of Mathematics 5–14.

Using the assessment materials

The *Check-ups*, *Topic Assessments* and *Round-up* provide useful information on:
– an individual child's progress, noting areas of success and highlighting specific areas of difficulty
– how the class or groups of children are progressing, indicating success or common difficulties that have emerged which require attention.

For example, discussion with the children about their work on a particular *Check-up* may help to establish why specific questions proved difficult. From this discussion important teaching points may be identified.

One copy of the *Check-ups* could be used to record specific comments about common difficulties. For example, using a highlighter pen to indicate questions where a significant number of children had experienced difficulty, or by circling questions where no errors occurred.

Recording progress

Assessment record grid

An assessment record grid is provided on page 48 of this guide to help record class, group or individual coverage of the *Check-ups*, *Topic Assessments* and *Round-up* completed. Ways of recording coverage might include a tick (✓) or a qualitative indicator of how well a specific assessment was completed. This could be done by shading part or all of an individual box. For example:

- ☐ no errors made
- ◩ few errors made
- ■ a significant number of errors made.

Level D class record grid

Pages 51–52 provide a simple checklist of all the attained targets for Level D. Space is provided to note work which has been attempted and the quality of the performances of the individuals within the class. It enables the teacher to monitor the progress of the whole class.

Record of work grids

Record of work grids are provided on pages 53–55 of this *Organising and Planning Guide*. These grids can be used to show:
- when work has been completed
- how well the work has been completed, for example by using a code as above.

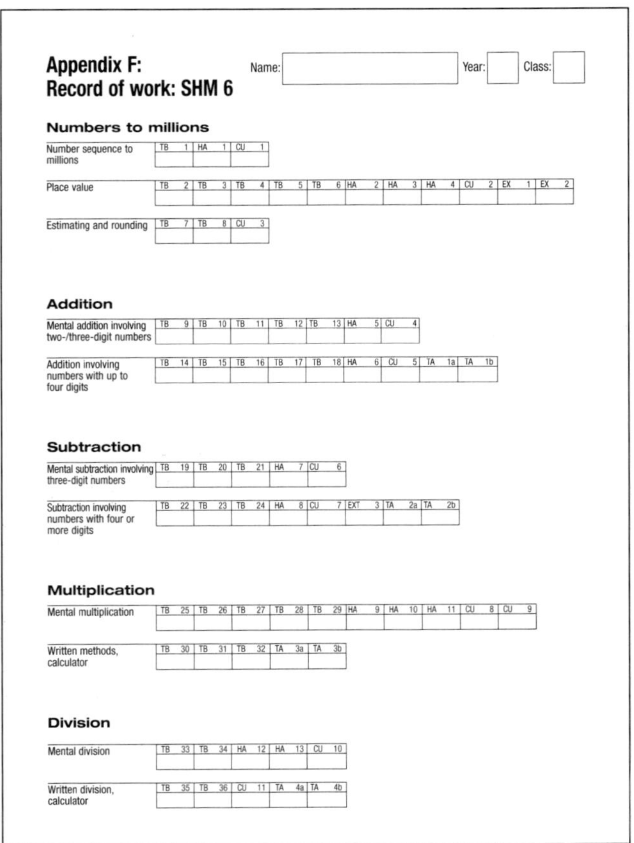

Appendix F:
Record of work: SHM 6

Name: _______ Year: ___ Class: ___

Numbers to millions

Number sequence to millions

TB 1	HA 1	CU 1

Place value

TB 2	TB 3	TB 4	TB 5	TB 6	HA 2	HA 3	CU 2	EX 1	EX 2

Estimating and rounding

TB 7	TB 8	CU 3

Addition

Mental addition involving two-/three-digit numbers

TB 9	TB 10	TB 11	TB 12	TB 13	HA 5	CU 4

Addition involving numbers with up to four digits

TB 14	TB 15	TB 16	TB 17	TB 18	HA 6	CU 5	TA 1a	TA 1b

Subtraction

Mental subtraction involving three-digit numbers

TB 19	TB 20	TB 21	HA 7	CU 6

Subtraction involving numbers with four or more digits

TB 22	TB 23	TB 24	HA 8	CU 7	EXT 3	TA 2a	TA 2b

Multiplication

Mental multiplication

TB 25	TB 26	TB 27	TB 28	TB 29	HA 9	HA 10	HA 11	CU 8	CU 9

Written methods, calculator

TB 30	TB 31	TB 32	TA 3a	TA 3b

Division

Mental division

TB 33	TB 34	HA 12	HA 13	CU 10

Written division, calculator

TB 35	TB 36	CU 11	TA 4a	TA 4b

Appendices

Appendix A: Development planner

Unit	Mathematics 5–14	SHM Topic

Information handling 1	**C/D**
	• **By selecting sources of information** for tasks, including a questionnaire which allows several responses to each question.
	O/D
	• **By using diagrams or tables.**
	D/D
	• **By constructing graphs (bar, line, frequency polygon) and pie charts:**
	  – involving simple fractions or decimals
	  – involving continuous data which has been grouped.
	I/D
	• **From a range of displays and databases** by retrieving information subject to one condition.
		Data Handling
		• **Interpreting graphs/data**
		  – introduces trend graphs
		  – revises the range and mode of a set of data and introduces the median
		  – introduces the mean of a set of data
		  – introduces compound bar charts and considers how aspects of a set of data may be shown more clearly by a compound bar chart than by a bar chart, and vice versa
		  – introduces, in extension activities, simple pie charts, comparing their effectiveness with that of a compound bar chart and a bar line chart.
		• **Bar charts with class intervals**
		  – introduces bar charts with class intervals
		  – includes, as an extension activity, survey work with an emphasis on designing questionnaires.

Information handling 2	**C/D**
	• **By selecting sources of information** for tasks, including a questionnaire which allows several responses to each question.
	O/D
	• **By using a database or spreadsheet table** with up to three fields defined by pupils.
	I/D
	• **From a range of displays and databases** by retrieving information subject to one condition.
		Data Handling
		• **Spreadsheets and databases**
		  – consolidates extracting information presented in tabular form
		  – develops entering data on a simple spreadsheet
		  – deals with interpreting information from a complex database.
		• **Language of probability**
		  – introduces language associated with the probability of an event occurring including:
		    – likelihood: impossible, unlikely, equally likely, likely and certain
		    – chance: no chance, poor chance, even chance, evens, good chance (and certain)
		  – begins to consider the meaning of fair and unfair.

Number 1	**RTN/D**
	• **Work with:**
	  – whole numbers up to 100 000 (count, order, read/write)
	  – whole numbers up to a million (read/write only).
	RN/D
	• **Round any number** to the nearest appropriate whole number, ten or hundred.
		Numbers to millions
		• **Number sequences to millions**
		  – Consolidates the number sequence to 100 thousands
		  – Develops the number sequence to millions (seven-/eight-digit numbers)
		  – Includes finding, in relation to ascending and descending sequences:
		    – the numbers 1, 2, 10, 50, 100, 500, 1000, 10 000, 100 000, 1 000 000 more/less than a given number
		    – multiples of 10, 100, 1000, 10 000, 100 000, 1 000 000.
		• **Place value**
		  – introduces place value for numbers with up to eight digits
		  – includes adding and subtracting mentally on a calculator, 10/100/1000/100 000/1 000 000 to and from numbers with up to eight digits
		  – introduces, as an extension activity, adding and subtracting mentally multiples of 1000/10000/100 000/1 000 000 to and from numbers with up to seven digits
		  – deals with
		    – identifying the larger/smaller number in a pair and the largest/smallest number in a set of up to five
		    – ordering up to five non-consecutive numbers
		    – finding the number halfway between a pair of multiples of 1 000 000 or 1 000 000
		    – reading and writing numbers to millions
		    – revises mental multiplication of a two-/three-/four-digit number by 10 and a two-/three-digit number by 100
		    – introduces mental multiplication of a two-/three-/four-digit number by 1000
		    – develops mental division to 10, 100 and 1000 of appropriate powers to 10 to include numbers with up to six digits
		    – introduces work with ancient Egyptian number symbols as an extension activity.
		• **Estimating and rounding**
		  – revise estimating the position on a number line of
		    – a multiple of 100 on a 0–1000 line
		    – a multiple of 20 on a 0–200 line
		  and extends this to a multiple of 1000 or 2500 on a 0–10 000 line

	SHM Resources				Assessment		Other resources	Date	Comment
Teaching File page	Textbook	Extension Textbook	Pupil Sheet	Home Activity	Check-up	Topic Assessment			
364–371	113–117	E20–E21							
372–375	118	E22	56–57						
378–382	119–122		58						
383–386	123					15			
42–46	1		1–3	1	1				
47–59	2–6	E1–E2	4–8	2–4	2				
60–66	7–8		9		3				

Appendix A: Development planner

Unit	Mathematics 5–14	SHM Topic
Number 1 (cont.)		– includes problem solving activities which involve estimating quantities – introduces rounding a five-/six-digit number to the nearest 1000/100 and a seven-/eight-digit number to the nearest million.

Number 2	AS/D
	● **Add:**
	  – mentally for 2 digit whole numbers, beyond in some cases, involving multiples of 10 or 100
	  – without a calculator, for 4 digits with at most two decimal places
	  – with a calculator, for 4 digits with at most two decimal places.
		Addition
		● **Mental addition involving two-/three-digit numbers**
		  – consolidates and develops strategies for metal addition of several two-digit numbers
		  – introduces finding an approximate total based on rounding three-digit numbers to the nearest hundred/nearest ten
		  – consolidates mental addition of three-digit numbers, bridging a multiple of 10, for example: 428 + 267, 149 + ■ = 682
		  – introduces mental addition of three-digit numbers
		    – bridging a multiple of 100, for example: 493 + 272, 193 + ■ = 753
		    – bridging 1000, for example: 635 + 853, 650 + ■ = 1170
		  – introduces the use of a doubling strategy for mental addition of two numbers close to and on either side of the same multiple of 100, for example: 421 + 387.
		● **Addition involving numbers with up to four digits**
		  – introduces mental addition of four-digit multiples of 100, for example: 6100 + 2300, 4400 + 3800, 6500 + 7600
		  – introduces mental addition of four-digit numbers with no bridging (2634 + 2352) then bridging a multiple of 10 only (4564 + 2107)
		  – further develops the use of a standard written method of addition of:
		    – two numbers with four digits
		    – several numbers with different numbers of digits
		    to include totals greater than 10 000.

Number 3	AS/D
	● **Subtract:**
	  – mentally for 2 digit whole numbers, beyond in some cases, involving multiples of 10 or 100
	  – without a calculator, for 4 digits with at most two decimal places
	  – with a calculator, for 4 digits with at most two decimal places.
		Subtraction
		● **Mental subtraction involving three-digit numbers**
		  – revises mental subtraction of a two-digit number from a three-digit number
		  – revises mental subtraction involving three-digit multiples of 10 (550 − 260) and introduces mental subtraction, bridging a multiple of 100:
		    – of a three-digit multiple of 10 from any three-digit number (768 − 380)
		    – of any three-digit number from a three-digit multiple of 10 (650 − 464)
		  – introduces mental subtraction of three-digit numbers, bridging a multiple of 10 (862 − 349).
		● **Subtraction involving numbers with four or more digits**
		  – revises mental subtraction from a four-digit multiple of 100 and then from any four-digit number of a three-digit multiple of 100 (4300 − 600 → 8197 − 500)
		  – introduces mental subtraction from a four-digit multiple of 100 of
		    – another four-digit multiple of 100, bridging a multiple of 1000 (7300 − 6800)
		    – a four-digit multiple of 50, not bridging a multiple of 1000 (8400 - 5150)
		  – introduces mental subtraction from a multiple of 1000 of any three-/four-digit number (2000 − 754, 8000 − 2785)
		  – introduces mental subtraction from a four-digit number of a three-/four-digit number
		    – with no bridging (3956 − 703, 7568 − 1352)
		    – bridging a multiple of 10 only (2894 − 745, 6722 − 2607)
		  – consolidates a standard written method of subtraction and includes subtractions involving
		    – four-digit numbers (9672 − 4883)
		    – different numbers of digits (3215 − 76)
		  – provides opportunities to use and apply skills in mental subtraction and in using a calculator
		  – provides an extension activity dealing with using a calculator for **addition and subtraction** of numbers with more than four digits.

Number 4	MD/D
	● **Multiply:**
	  – mentally for whole numbers by single digits
	  – mentally for four-digit numbers including decimals by 10 or 100
	  – without a calculator for 4 digits with at most 2 decimal places by a single digit
	  – with a calculator for 4 digits with at most 2 decimal places by a whole number with 2 digits
	  in applications in number, measurement and money.
		Multiplication
		● **Mental multiplication**
		  – revises multiplication facts for 2 to 10 and finding mentally products involving multiples of 10/100/1000, for example: 20 × 9, 400 × 8, 6 × 3000, 40 × 700
		  – revises multiplying a two-digit number by a single digit with bridging, for example:
		    6×37 ⟨ $6 \times 30 = 180$; $6 \times 7 = 42$ ⟩ $180 + 42 = 222$
		  – revises a range of mental multiplication strategies based on the distributive property and/or doubling/halving:
		    – using doubling to build up a 'multiplication table' for a two-digit number

SHM Resources					Assessment		Other resources	Date	Comment
Teaching File page	Textbook	Extension Textbook	Pupil Sheet	Home Activity	Check-up	Topic Assessment			
70–77	9–13		10	5	4				
78–83	14–18			6	5	1a, b			
90–95	19–21			7	6				
96–103	22–24	3	11–12	8	7	2a, b			
112–122	25–29		13–15	9–10	8–9				

Appendix A: Development planner

Unit	Mathematics 5–14	SHM Topic
Number 4 (cont.)		– doubling a number ending in 5 and halving the other number, for example: $15 \times 16 \rightarrow 30 \times 8 = 240$ – halving an even teens number and doubling another number, for example: $14 \times 23 \rightarrow 7 \times 46 = 322$ – introduces mental multiplication strategies based on multiplying by 100, for example: – multiplying by 50 by multiplying by 100 then halving: $50 \times 23 \rightarrow 100 \times 23$ (2300) $\rightarrow$ half of 2300 = 1150 – multiplying by 25 by multiplying by 100, halving and then halving again: $25 \times 32 \rightarrow 100 \times 32$ (3200) $\rightarrow$ half of 3200 (1600) $\rightarrow$ half of 1600 = 800 – introduces mental multiplication of a two-digit number by 99, 101/49, 51 by multiplying by 100/50 then adjusting – introduces using factors as a strategy for multiplying a pair of two-digit numbers – uses and applies knowledge of multiplication facts and strategies to solve number problems. ● **Written methods, calculator** – develops an informal written method for multiplication of a one-digit number by a single digit – uses an expanded vertical recording which leads to the further development of a standard written method of multiplication of a four-digit number by a single digit – consolidates informal and standard written methods for multiplication of a two-digit number by a two-digit number – provides opportunities for using and applying knowledge and skills in multiplication – includes multiplication of three-/four-digit numbers by a two-digit number using a calculator.
Number 5	**MD/D** ● **Divide:** – mentally for whole numbers by single digits – mentally for four-digit numbers including decimals by 10 or 100 – without a calculator for 4 digits with at most 2 decimal places by a single digit – with a calculator for 4 digits with at most 2 decimal places by a whole number with 2 digits in applications in number, measurement and money.	**Division** ● **Mental division** – revises mental division based on tables facts, including remainders – consolidates and develops work on finding mentally half of – any three-digit even number – four-digit multiples of 10 to 2000 (examples with an even tens digit only i.e. finding half of 1940 but not 1730) – four-digit multiples of 100 (examples with an even hundreds digit only i.e. finding half of 5800 but not 7500) – introduces mental strategies for division by a single digit of – certain three-digit multiples of 10 ($320 \div 8 \rightarrow 32 \div 8 = 4$, $320 \div 8 = \mathbf{40}$) – numbers just beyond the extent of the tables ($52 \div 4 \rightarrow 52 = 40 + 12$, $40 \div 4 = 10$, $12 \div 4 = 3$, so $52 \div 4 = \mathbf{13}$ (10 + 3)) – certain three-digit numbers, based on tables facts ($763 \div 7 \rightarrow 700 \div 7 = 100$, $63 \div 7 = 9$, $763 \div 7 = \mathbf{109}$) – includes, in an extension activity, division word problems involving one million. ● **Written division, calculator** – revises and develops division, exact and with remainders, of a three-digit number by a single digit using: – a short standard written method based on place value sharing – an alternative written method involving repeated subtraction of multiples of the divisor (two- and three-digit quotients) – introduces (using the **school's choice** of written method) division, exact and with remainders, of a four-digit number by a single digit (three- and four-digit quotients).
Number 6	**PS/D** ● **Continue and describe more complex sequences.** **FE/D** ● **Recognise and explain simple relationships:** – between two sets of numbers or objects. **MD/D** ● **Multiply and divide:** – mentally for whole numbers by single digits.	**Number properties** ● **Number sequences and patterns** – consolidates continuing number sequences and using 'rules' to describe or generate number sequences, including sequences which: – increase or decrease in single-digit steps and in steps of 11/15/19/21/25 – involve doubling/halving – consolidates language (square, squared) and notation ($25 = 5 \times 5 = 5^2$) associated with square numbers and introduces, in a follow-up activity, the idea of a square root. – explores types of numbers in investigations which lead to generalisations about products of odd/even numbers, for example, 'the product of two odd/even numbers is an odd/even number' – investigates, in extension activities: – ordering and addition and subtraction of negative numbers, in the context of temperature – identifying and continuing number patterns.

SHM Resources					Assessment		Other resources	Date	Comment
Teaching File page	Textbook	Extension Textbook	Pupil Sheet	Home Activity	Check-up	Topic Assessment			
123–128	30–32		16–17			3a, b			
134–140	33–34		18–19	12–13	10				
141–145	35–36		20–22		11	4a, b			
152–163	37–39	4–6	23–24	14					

Appendix A: Development planner

Unit	Mathematics 5–14	SHM Topic

Number 6 (cont.)		**● Divisibility, multiples and factors, word formulae**
		– revises methods (which involve consideration of the last digit/s or the digit sum) of 'testing' numbers, without dividing, for exact divisibility by 2, 3, 4, 5, 9, 10 and 100
		– introduces methods (which involve a 'two-step' process) of testing numbers without dividing, for divisibility by 4, 6 and 8, for example: 168 is exactly divisible by 8 because half of it, 84 (168 ÷ 2), is exactly divisible by 4
		– consolidates multiples and common multiples and introduces the idea of a smallest/lowest common multiple for a pair of numbers, for example: 3 and 4, 10 and 15, 4 and 16
		– consolidates factors, including finding all the factor pairs of a number and listing all its factors, and by investigating sets of numbers leads to the discoveries that:
		  – a square number has an odd number of factors
		  – a prime number has only two factors, itself and 1
		– introduces finding the 'rule' or word formula to describe a relationship between two sets of numbers
		– uses and applies knowledge of number properties to solve a range of problems and puzzles.

Number 7	**RTN/D**
	● Work with:
	– fractions (all previous plus twentieths, fiftieths, hundredths) and equivalences among these and decimals (in applications).
	FPR/D
	● Work with fractions and percentages
	– find simple fractions ($\frac{1}{7}$, $\frac{3}{4}$, $\frac{3}{5}$, $\frac{60}{100}$) of quantities involving at most 4 digits (easy examples only).
		Fractions
		● Equivalence
		– consolidates proper/improper fraction language and the conversion of mixed numbers to improper fractions and vice versa
		– revises forming equivalent fractions by multiplying numerator and denominator and extends this to *any* fraction
		– introduces forming equivalent fractions by dividing numerator and denominator and associated language (simplifying, simplest form)
		– deals with comparing and ordering fractions with different denominators
		– includes, as an extension activity, informal addition and subtraction of fractions and mixed numbers involving quarters, halves and three quarters.
		● Fraction of a set/quantity; hundredths
		– consolidates finding a fraction, numerator = 1, of a set
		– introduces fractional notation, including mixed numbers, for hundredths
		– introduces finding 'any' fraction, numerator ≥ 1, of a set/quantity, for example: $\frac{3}{7}$ of 21, $\frac{7}{100}$ of 500, $\frac{4}{9}$ of 45 m; $\frac{2}{5}$ of 2 kg, including finding several hundredths of £1, 1 m, 1 km, 1 kg and 1ℓ, for example: $\frac{9}{100}$ of 1 km, $\frac{6}{100}$ ℓ
		– develops expressing one quantity as a fraction of another to include
		  – for tenths, quantities greater than £1 and 1 m, for example: expressing £1.30 as £1$\frac{3}{10}$, 180 cm as 1$\frac{8}{10}$ m
		  – pence, cm, m, g and ml as hundredths of £1, 1 m, 1 km, 1 kg and 1ℓ respectively, for example: expressing 20 m as $\frac{2}{100}$ km, 70 ml as $\frac{7}{100}$ ℓ.

Number 8	**RTN/D** **● Work with** fractions (all previous plus twentieths, fiftieths, hundredths) and equivalences among these and decimals (in applications). **AS/D** ● Without a calculator, for 4 digits with at most two decimal places ● With a calculator, for 4 digits with at most two decimal places.	**Decimals** **● Tenths** – revises decimal notation for tenths in two- and three-digit numbers, for example: 2·6, 27·9 – links the decimal notation to the corresponding notation for fractions and mixed numbers, for example: $\frac{3}{10}$ → 0·3, 2$\frac{7}{10}$ → 2·7 – includes work on place value, sequences, comparing and ordering two- and three-digit decimals – deals with mental methods for adding and subtracting two-digit decimals, for example: 1·7 + 5·6, 7·2 – 3·9 – uses standard written methods for adding and subtracting three-digit decimals, for example: 57·5 + 38·4, 93·9 – 77·2 – deals with the mental multiplication of a two-digit number with one decimal place by a single digit – introduces multiplication of a three-digit number with one decimal place by a single digit, using informal and standard written methods – introduces mental division of a one- or two-digit number by 10 – introduces mental division of a two-digit number with one decimal place by a single digit – introduces division of a three-digit number with one decimal place by a single digit using a standard written method.

| Teaching File page | SHM Resources | | | | Assessment | | Other resources | Date | Comment |
	Textbook	Extension Textbook	Pupil Sheet	Home Activity	Check-up	Topic Assessment			
164–175	40–47		25			5a, b			
182–190	48–50	10	26–28	15	12				
191–198	51–53		29	16	13	6a, b			
208–220	54–60		30–35	17–18	14–16				

Appendix A: Development planner

Unit	Mathematics 5–14	SHM Topic

Number 9	**RTN/D**
	● **Work with** decimals to 2 place and equivalences among these in applications in money and measurement.
	AS/D
	● Without a calculator, for 4 digits with at most two decimal places
	● With a calculator, for 4 digits with at most two decimal places.
		Decimals
		● **Hundredths**
		– introduces decimal notation for hundredths in numbers with up to four digits
		– includes linking decimal notation to the corresponding notation for fractions and mixed numbers, for example: $0{\cdot}39 \to \frac{39}{100}$, $46{\cdot}2 \to 46\frac{2}{10} \to 46\frac{1}{5}$ or $46\frac{20}{100}$
		– deals with place value for one- and two-place decimals with up to four digits and includes recognising:
		  – the larger/smaller decimal in a pair of numbers
		  – the largest/smallest decimal in a set of 3 numbers
		  – the two-place decimal before/after/between
		– includes ordering sets of up to six one-/two-place decimals with up to three digits, and simple sequences
		– introduces addition and subtraction of two-place decimals using mental strategies (for three-digit numbers) and standard written methods (for three-/four-digit numbers)
		– uses and applies decimal notation in the contexts of length, for example: 3·67 m and money, for example: £12·02
		– introduces mental multiplication of a two-/three-digit number with one/two decimal places by 10, 100 or a multiple of 10
		– includes using and applying calculator skills to solve problems involving decimals
		– introduces, in extension activities, multiplication and division of a three-digit number with one/two decimal places using standard written methods.

Number 10	**RTN/D** ● **Work with:** percentages, decimals to 2 places and equivalences among these in applications in money and measurement. **FPR/D** ● **Work with fractions and percentages:** – find simple fractions ($\frac{1}{7}$, $\frac{3}{4}$, $\frac{3}{5}$, $\frac{60}{100}$) of quantities involving at most 4 digits (easy examples only).	**Percentages** ● **Percentages** – introduces the concept of percentages – introduces the links between fractions, decimals, and percentages, for example: $\frac{20}{100} = 0{\cdot}20 = 20\%$ – deals with finding the percentage of a shape which is shaded – includes finding a percentage of a set/quantity.
Measure 1	**T/D** ● **Work with time:** – use 24-hour times and equate with 12-hour times.	**Time** ● **Reading and writing times** – revises reading times in 1 minute intervals on analogue and digital displays – revises writing times in 1 minute intervals using 12-hour notation and am/pm – introduces reading and writing times in 1 minute intervals using 24-hour notation.

Measure 2	**T/D**
	● **Work with time:**
	– use 24-hour times and equate with 12-hour times
	– calculate duration in hours/minutes, mentally if possible
	– time activities in seconds with a stopwatch
	– calculate speeds.
		Time
		● **Durations, seconds**
		– introduces finding times in multiples of 5 minutes before/after times displayed in 24-hour notation:
		  – bridging one hour, for example: 25 min after 08:55
		  – bridging more than an hour, for example 1h and 50 min after 22:30
		– introduces finding durations in multiples of 5 minutes between digital times given in 24-hour notation, bridging one hour/more than one hour
		– includes problems which require the children to use and apply the above
		– deals with estimating and measuring activities involving units of time
		– deals with seconds and using and reading stopclocks in practical estimating and measuring activities
		– introduces *rate* as an extension

Measure 3	**ME/D**
	● **Measure in standard units:**
	– length: small lengths in millimetres; large lengths like buildings in metres.
	● **Recognise** when kilometres are appropriate.
		Measure
		● **Length**
		– consolidates estimating and measuring lengths in metres and centimetres
		– includes activities involving:
		  – the millimetre and the relationship 10 mm = 1 cm
		  – the kilometre and the relationship with metres, for example: 1 km = 1 000 m, $\frac{1}{10}$ km = 100 m and $\frac{3}{4}$ km = 750 m
		– involves using practical skills to choose appropriate units and measuring devices and applying knowledge to solve problems
		– introduces finding the perimeters of shapes by adding the lengths and their sides and introduces word formulae for finding the perimeter of a rectangle and a regular polygon.

| Teaching File page | SHM Resources | | | | Assessment | | Other resources | Date | Comment |
	Textbook	Extension Textbook	Pupil Sheet	Home Activity	Check-up	Topic Assessment			
221–232	61–68	8–9	36–37	19–21		7a, b			
240–249	69–72	11	38–39	22		8a, b			
256–260	73–74		41	23					
261–266	75–78	12–13	42–43			9			
272–280	79–84		44			10			

Appendix A: Development planner

Unit	Mathematics 5–14	SHM Topic
Measure 4	**ME/D** ● **Measure in standard units:** – weight: extended range of articles, for example own weight. ● **Estimate** small weights in easily handled units. ● **Select appropriate measuring devices and units** for weight.	**Measure** ● **Weight** – revises reading scales marked in 10 g, 20 g, 50 g and 100 g divisions – introduces reading and recording weights to the nearest mark on scales showing tenths of a kilogram in decimal form (0.1 kg) and in multiples of 100 g – revises recording in grams weights given in kilograms and grams and vice versa, for example: 4kg 125 g → 4125 g, 3697 g → 3 kg 697 g – uses and applies knowledge of weight in practical contexts.
Measure 5	**ME/C** ● **Measure in standard units:** – volume: accuracy extended to small containers in millilitres; 1 ℓ = 1000 ml – temperature. ● **Estimate** small volumes in easily handled units. ● **Be aware of common Imperial units** in appropriate practical applications.	**Measure** ● **Volume/Capacity** – revises the relationships 1 ℓ = 1000 ml, $\frac{1}{2}\ell$ = 500ml, $\frac{1}{4}\ell$ = 250ml and $\frac{3}{4}\ell$ = 750ml – introduces the tenth of a litre and the relationships $\frac{1}{10}\ell$ = 100ml, $\frac{2}{10}\ell$ = 200ml… – revises reading scales marked in 100ml, 50ml, 20ml and 10ml divisions – provides practical estimating and measuring activities and includes solving problems in non-practical situations – introduces, in a problem solving activity, the relationship: *1 cm³ has the same volume as 1 ml.* ● **Mixed measure** – deals with commonly used Imperial units – the mile, pint and gallon – and their approximate metric equivalents – includes problems involving weight, volume/capacity, temperature and time.
Measure 6	**ME/C** ● **Measure in standard units:** – area: right-angled triangles on cm squared grids. ● **Estimate** small areas in easily handed standard units.	**Measure** ● **Area** – revises using the formula in words for finding the area of a rectangle and introduces expressing this in letters as A=l×b – applies the formula, A=l×b, to rectangles with side lengths in half centimetres – introduces finding the approximate area of squares and rectangles to the nearest cm² – provides practice in finding the approximate areas of irregular shapes – develops finding the area, in cm² and m², of a simple composite shape sub-divided into rectangles – introduces finding the area of a right-angled triangle drawn on a squared grid – consolidates a counting method for finding the area of an irregular shape drawn on a dotty grid in square units and half-square units – includes problems which require the children to use and apply the above – develops, in an extension activity, methods for **calculating** the area of a right-angled triangle.
Shape 1	**S/D** ● **Work with symmetry:** – identify and draw lines of symmetry, generally up to 4 – create symmetrical shapes.	**2D Shape** ● **Line symmetry** – revises reflecting simple shapes in mirror lines in a variety of orientations – develops sketching the reflection of a shape in one line of symmetry where at least two sides of the shape are not parallel to or perpendicular to the line of symmetry – introduces reflecting straight and then curved lines to create patterns with both horizontal and vertical lines of symmetry.

Shape 2	**RS/D**
	● **Collect, discuss, make and use 2D shapes:**
	– discuss 2D shapes referring to sides, diagonals, angles
	– recognise pentagon, hexagon
	– identify and name equilateral and isosceles triangles
	– extend shape vocabulary to radius, diameter, circumference
	– create or copy a tiling using a shape template
	– use the rigidity property of triangles in model-making.
		2D Shape
		● **Properties, puzzles and patterns**
		– consolidates naming and describing triangles, quadrilaterals and other polygons using side and angle properties
		– revises equilateral and isosceles triangles and introduces scalene and right-angled triangles
		– introduces the parallelogram, rhombus, trapezium and kite, extending the language of shape to include the terms adjacent sides, opposite sides/angles
		– introduces further work on tiling patterns drawn on squared and isometric dotty grids
		– introduces using compasses to draw a variety of circle designs
		– includes, in extension activities, investigations involving:
		  – the rigidity property of the triangle
		  – the seven-piece Tangram
		  – drawing pursuit curve patterns in a range of triangles, quadrilaterals and regular polygons
		  – exploring number patterns arising when intersecting straight lines are drawn between points.

| Teaching File page | SHM Resources | | | | Assessment | | Other resources | Date | Comment |
	Textbook	Extension Textbook	Pupil Sheet	Home Activity	Check-up	Topic Assessment			
284–288	85–86		45–46			11			
292–296	87–90		47–48						
297–299	91–92								
302–312	93–97	E19	49–50						
320–326	98		51–52						
327–334	99–104	E14–E18	53–54			13a, b			

Appendix A: Development planner

Unit	Mathematics 5–14	SHM Topic

Shape 3	**RS/D**
	● **Collect, discuss, make and use 3D shapes:**
	  – discuss 3D shapes referring to faces, edges, vertices
	  – make 3D models, solid or skeletal, including using nets: cube and cuboid only.
		3D Shape
		● **3D Shape**
		  – explores possible nets of a cube
		  – includes identifying shapes from their nets
		  – introduces finding the total surface area of various 3D shapes
		  – consolidates and develops work on interpreting 2D representations of 3D shapes composed of linking cubes.

Shape 4	**PM/D**
	● **Discuss position and movement:**
	  – give directions for a route or journey
	  – use and 8-point compass rose
	  – use a co-ordinate system to locate a point on a grid
	  – create patterns by rotating a shape.
	A/D
	● **Angles:**
	  – draw, copy and measure angles accurately within 5 degrees
	  – use standard notation, 060°, 150°, 300°, to express bearings.
		Shape
		● **Position, movement and angle**
		  – uses the 8-point compass and a 12-point dial respectively to consolidate in multiples of 45° and 30°
		  – introduces bearings and the associated three-figure notation, for example 090°
		  – introduces drawing, on a squared grid, shapes which have been rotated through 90°, 180° and 270° and includes locating the positions of the vertices of shapes on a co-ordinate grid, before and after rotation
		  – introduces estimating and measuring angles to the nearest 5°.

Teaching File page	SHM Resources				Assessment		Other resources	Date	Comment
	Textbook	Extension Textbook	Pupil Sheet	Home Activity	Check-up	Topic Assessment			
340–346	105–108								
350–358	109–112		55			14a, b			

Appendix B: Block planner   Year:

Class: **Group:**   **Block 1**   **Date:**

WEEK	ORAL/MENTAL	MATHEMATICS TOPIC
1	• **Adding/subtracting powers of 10 to/from numbers with up to 8 digits** • **Multiplying/dividing by 10, 100 and 1000**	**Number unit 1:** Numbers to millions
2		
3		
4		**Measure unit 3:** Length
5		**Shape unit 1:** 2D Shape: line symmetry
6		**Measure unit 4:** Weight

Class: **Group:**   **Block 2**   **Date:**

WEEK	ORAL/MENTAL	MATHEMATICS TOPIC
1	• **Adding two-/three-digit numbers** • **Adding four-digit multiples of 100**	**Number unit 2:** Addition
2		
3	• **Subtracting two-/three-digit numbers** • **Subtracting from four-digit multiples of 100 and 1000**	**Number unit 3:** Subtraction
4		
5		**Measure unit 1:** Time: reading and writing times
6		**Shape unit 2:** 2D Shape: properties, puzzles and patterns

Appendix B: Block planner   Year:

Class: **Group:**   **Block 3**   **Date:**

WEEK	ORAL/MENTAL	MATHEMATICS TOPIC
1	• Tables facts • Multiplying by multiples of 10, 100 and 1000 • Multiplying a two-digit number by a single digit • Multiplication strategies	**Number unit 4:** Multiplication
2		
3		
4		**Measure unit 6:** Area
5		**Data Handling unit 1:** Interpreting graphs/data
6		

Class: **Group:**   **Block 4**   **Date:**

WEEK	ORAL/MENTAL	MATHEMATICS TOPIC
1	• Division facts • Halving three-/four-digit numbers • Dividing numbers 'beyond the tables' by a single digit	**Number unit 5:** Division
2		
3		
4	• Continuing number sequences • Using 'rules' to describe or generate number sequences • 'Testing' numbers for exact divisibility by 2, 3, 4, 5, 6, 8, 9, 10 and 100	**Number unit 6:** Number Properties
5		
6		**Measure unit 2:** Time: durations, seconds **Shape unit 3:** 3D Shape

Appendix B: Block planner

Year:

Class: **Group:**   **Block 5**   **Date:**

WEEK	ORAL/MENTAL	MATHEMATICS TOPIC
1	• Converting mixed numbers to improper fractions and vice versa	**Number unit 7:** Fractions
2	• Forming equivalent fractions by multiplying/dividing numerator and denominator	
3	• Adding/subtracting two-digit numbers with one decimal place	**Number unit 8:** Decimals: tenths
4	• Multiplying/dividing two-digit numbers with one decimal place by a single digit	
5		**Measure unit 5:** Volume/Capacity
6		**Shape unit 4:** Position, Movement and Angle

Class: **Group:**   **Block 6**   **Date:**

WEEK	ORAL/MENTAL	MATHEMATICS TOPIC
1	• Adding/subtracting three-digit numbers with two decimal places	**Number unit 9:** Decimals: hundredths
2	• Multiplying two-/three-digit numbers with one/two decimal place/s by 10 and 100	
3		
4	• Expressing percentages in decimal/fractional form and vice versa	**Number unit 10:** Percentages
5	• Finding a percentage of a set/quantity	
6		**Data Handling unit 2:** Spreadsheets and databases, Language of probability

Appendix B: Block planner

Year:

Class: **Group:**   **Block**   **Date:**

WEEK	ORAL/MENTAL	MATHEMATICS TOPIC
1		
2		
3		
4		
5		
6		

Class: **Group:**   **Block**   **Date:**

WEEK	ORAL/MENTAL	MATHEMATICS TOPIC
1		
2		
3		
4		
5		
6		

Appendix C: Development charts

Problem-solving and enquiry

Problem-solving and enquiry activities are included throughout the materials. These activities challenge children to think, to question and to explain.

Data Handling	Number						
	Counting and place value	Addition & Subtraction	Multiplication & Division	Number Properties	Fractions	Decimals	Percentages
SHM 5							
– revises simple frequency axis scales – introduces bar line charts – extracting information – databases – spreadhseets – mean/average	**Numbers to 100 thousands** – number sequence to 10 000 – place value, comparing and ordering – number names, ordinal numbers	**Addition** – doubles/near doubles – involving three-digit numbers – involving four-digit numbers **Addition beyond 1000** – mental strategies **Subtraction** – mental subtraction, two-digit numbers – mental subtraction, three-digit numbers – written methods **Subtraction beyond 1000** – mental strategies	**Multiplication** – by 10, 100 – mental strategies – written strategies – using doubles – written methods **Division** – by 1–10, 100, 1000 – halving; linking multiplication and division – three-digit numbers, remainders	**Number properties** – number patterns and sequences – factors – square numbers – negative numbers	**Fractions** – halves, quarters, tenths, thirds and fifths – of a shape – equivalence – of a set/quantity	**Decimals** – tenths	
SHM 6							
– introduces trends graphs – revises the range and mode – introduces the median and the mean – introduces compound bar graphs – introduces simple pie charts	**Numbers to millions** – number sequence to millions – place value – estimating and rounding	**Addition** – mental addition involving two-/three-digit numbers – involving numbers with up to four digits **Subtraction** – mental subtraction involving three-digit numbers – involving numbers with four or more digits	**Multiplication** – mental multiplication – written methods, calculator **Division** – mental division – written division, calculator	**Number properties** – number sequences and patterns – divisibility, multiples and factors, word formulae	**Fractions** – equivalence – fractions of a set/quantity; hundredths	**Decimals** – tenths – hundredths	**Percentages** – concept – links between fractions, decimals and percentages – percentages of shapes – of a set/quantity

	Measure				Shape		
Time	Length	Weight	Volume/Capacity	Area	3D Shape	2D Shape	Position, Movement & Angle
SHM 5							
– reading and writing times in 5 minute intervals – introduces reading and writing times in 1 minute intervals – durations	– measuring in metres and centimetres – estimating and measuring lengths to the nearest quarter-metre – recording in decimal form – measuring and drawing lengths – choosing appropriate units and instruments – the kilometre – perimeter	– the kilogram/gram relationship – recording weights – estimating and weighing – reading scales – weighing and recording to the nearest 100 g	– litres, half-litres and quarter litres – recording notation – scale reading – the cubic centimetre – finding volumes	– finding area in square centimetres – formula for area of a rectangle – finding approximate areas of irregular shapes – the square metre	– recognising and naming 3D shapes – the octahedron – 3D shape properties	– properties – line symmetry – tiling and patterns	– co-ordinates – drawing shapes (including symmetrical) on a co-ordinate grid – moving shapes on a squared grid – following and describing pathways – the 8-point compass – acute and obtuse angles
SHM 6							
– analogue and digital displays – 12-hour notation and am/pm – 24-hour notation – duration – estimating and measuring – rate	– estimating and measuring – relationships: mm/cm, km/m – perimeters	– reading scales – recording and recording – relationships: kg/g – practical contexts	– relationships: ml/ℓ – tenth of a litre – reading scales – estimating and measuring – Imperial units	– A = l×b – approximate areas of squares, rectangles and irregular shapes – simple composite shapes – right-angled triangles	– nets of a cube – identifying shapes from their nets – surface area – 2D representations of 3D shapes	– line symmetry – reflections where at least two sides are not parallel or perpendicular to line of symmetry – reflecting straight and curved lines – naming and using side and angle properties – equilateral, isosceles and right-angled triangles – adjacent sides – tiling patterns – circle designs – seven-piece Tangram – pursuit curves	– 8-point compass and 12-point dial; multiples of 45° and 30° – bearings and three-figure notation – drawing rotations – estimating and measuring angles

Appendix D: Assessment record grid

Year: ☐ Class: ☐

Topic Assessment

- Addition
- Subtraction
- Multiplication
- Division
- Number Properties
- Fractions
- Decimals
- Percentages
- Time
- Length
- Weight
- Area
- 2D Shape
- Position, Movement and Angle
- Data Handling
- Round-up Level D

Check-ups

- Numbers to millions: Check-up 1, Check-up 2, Check-up 3
- Addition: Check-up 4, Check-up 5
- Subtraction: Check-up 6, Check-up 7
- Multiplication: Check-up 8, Check-up 9
- Division: Check-up 10, Check-up 11
- Fractions: Check-up 12, Check-up 13
- Decimals: Check-up 14, Check-up 15, Check-up 16, Check-up 17, Check-up 18, Check-up 19

Names

Appendix E: Level D class record grid

Year: Class:

Names

Information Handling

Collect
- **By selecting sources of information** for tasks, including a questionnaire which allows several responses to each question.

Organise
- **By using diagrams or tables.**
- **By using a database or spreadsheet table** with up to three fields defined by pupils.
- With the aid, where appropriate, of a computer package.

Display
- **By constructing graphs (bar, line, frequency polygon) and pie charts.**
- Involving simple fractions or decimals.
- Involving continuous data which has been grouped.
- With the aid, where appropriate, of a computer package.

Interpret
- **From a range of displays and databases** by retrieving information subject to one condition.

Number, Money, Measure

Range and type of numbers
- **Work with** whole numbers up to 100 000 (count, order, read/write).
- **Work with** whole numbers up to a million (read/write only).
- **Work with** fractions (all previous plus twentieths, fiftieths, hundredths) and equivalences among these and decimals (in applications).
- **Work with** percentages, decimals to 2 places and equivalences among these in applications in money and measurement.

Money
- **Use all UK coins/notes** to £20 worth or more, including exchange.

Add
- Mentally for 2 digit whole numbers, beyond in some cases, involving multiples of 10 or 100.
- Without a calculator, for 4 digits with at most two decimal (easy examples only).
- With a calculator, for 4 digits with at most 2 decimal places.
- In applications in number, measurement and money.

Subtract
- Mentally for 2 digit whole numbers, beyond in some cases, involving multiples of 10 or 100.
- Without a calculator, for 4 digits with at most two decimal (easy examples only).
- With a calculator, for 4 digits with at most 2 decimal places.
- In applications in number, measurement and money.

Multiply
- Mentally for whole numbers by single digits: easy examples only.
- Mentally for 4 digit numbers including decimals by 10 or 100.
- Without a calculator for 4 digits with at most 2 decimal places by a whole number with 2 digits.
- In applications in number, measurement and money.

Divide
- Mentally for whole numbers by single digits: easy examples only.
- Mentally for 4 digit numbers including decimals by 10 or 100.
- Without a calculator for 4 digits with at most 2 decimal places by a whole number with 2 digits.
- In applications in number, measurement and money.

Appendix E: Level D class record grid

Year: ☐   Class: ☐

Names

Number, Money, Measure

Round Numbers
- **Round any number** to the nearest appropriate whole number, ten or hundred.

Fractions, Percentages and Ratio
- **Work with fractions and percentages:** find simple fractions ($\frac{1}{7}$, $\frac{3}{4}$, $\frac{3}{5}$, $\frac{60}{100}$) of quantities involving at most 4 digits (easy examples only).

Patterns and Sequences
- **Continue and describe more complex sequences.**

Functions and Equations
- **Recognise and explain simple relationships** between two sets of numbers or objects.

Measure and estimate
- **Measure in standard units:**
- – length: small lengths in millimetres; large lengths like buildings in metres.
- – weight: extended range of articles, for example own weight
- – volume: accuracy extended to small containers in millilitres; $1\,\ell = 1000\,ml$
- – area: right-angled triangles on cm squared grids
- – temperature.
- **Estimate** small weights, small areas, small volumes in easily handled standard units.
- **Recognise** when kilometres are appropriate.
- **Select appropriate measuring devices and units** for weight.
- **Be aware of common Imperial units** in appropriate practical applications.

Time
- Use 24-hour times and equate with 12-hour times.
- Calculate duration in hours/minutes, mentally if possible.
- Time activities in seconds with a stopwatch.
- Calculate speeds (practical activities only).

Perimeter, Formulae, Scales
- **Calculate perimeter** of simple straight-sided shapes by adding lengths.

Shape, Position and Movement

Range of shapes
Collect, discuss, make and use 3D and 2D shapes
- Discuss 3D and 2D shapes referring to faces, edges, vertices, diagonals, sides, angles.
- Recognise pentagon, hexagon.
- Identify and name equilateral and isosceles triangles.
- Extend shape vocabulary to radius, diameter, circumference.
- Create or copy a tiling using a shape template.
- Make 3D models, solid or skeletal, including using nets: cube and cuboid only.
- Use the rigidity property of triangles in model-making.

Position and movement
- Give directions for a route or journey.
- Use an 8 point compass rose.
- Use a co-ordinate system to locate a point on a grid.
- Create patterns by rotating a shape.

Symmetry
- Identify and draw lines of symmetry, generally up to 4.
- Create symmetrical shapes.

Angles
- Draw, copy and measure angles accurately within 5 degrees.
- Use standard notation, 060°, 150°, 300°, to express bearings.

Appendix F:
Record of work: SHM 6

Name: Year: Class:

Numbers to millions

Number sequence to millions		
TB 1	HA 1	CU 1

Place value										
TB 2	TB 3	TB 4	TB 5	TB 6	HA 2	HA 3	HA 4	CU 2	EX 1	EX 2

Estimating and rounding		
TB 7	TB 8	CU 3

Addition

Mental addition involving two-/three-digit numbers						
TB 9	TB 10	TB 11	TB 12	TB 13	HA 5	CU 4

Addition involving numbers with up to four digits								
TB 14	TB 15	TB 16	TB 17	TB 18	HA 6	CU 5	TA 1a	TA 1b

Subtraction

Mental subtraction involving three-digit numbers				
TB 19	TB 20	TB 21	HA 7	CU 6

Subtraction involving numbers with four or more digits							
TB 22	TB 23	TB 24	HA 8	CU 7	EXT 3	TA 2a	TA 2b

Multiplication

Mental multiplication									
TB 25	TB 26	TB 27	TB 28	TB 29	HA 9	HA 10	HA 11	CU 8	CU 9

Written methods, calculator				
TB 30	TB 31	TB 32	TA 3a	TA 3b

Division

Mental division				
TB 33	TB 34	HA 12	HA 13	CU 10

Written division, calculator				
TB 35	TB 36	CU 11	TA 4a	TA 4b

Appendix F:
Record of work: SHM 6

Name: Year: Class:

Number properties

Number sequences and patterns

TB 37	TB 38	TB 39	HA 14	EX 4	EX 5	EX 6

Divisibility, multiples and factors, word formulae

TB 40	TB 41	TB 42	TB 43	TB 44	TB 45	TB 46	TB 47	TA 5a	TA 5b

Fractions

Equivalence

TB 48	TB 49	TB 50	HA 15	CU 12	EX 10

Fraction of a set/quantity; hundredths

TB 51	TB 52	TB 53	HA 16	CU 13	TA 6a	TA 6b

Decimals

Tenths

TB 54	TB 55	TB 56	TB 57	TB 58	TB 59
TB 60	HA 17	HA 18	CU 14	CU 15	CU 16

Hundredths

TB 61	TB 62	TB 63	TB 64	TB 65	TB 66	TB 67	TB 68
HA 19	HA 20	HA 21	EX 8	EX 9	TA 7a	TA 7b	

Percentages

Percentages

TB 69	TB 70	TB 71	TB 72	HA 22	EX 11	TA 8a	TA 8b

Appendix F:
Record of work: SHM 6

Name: ______________ Year: ____ Class: ____

Measure

Time: reading and writing times	TB	73	TB	74	HA	23								

Time: durations, seconds	TB	75	TB	76	TB	77	TB	78	EX	12	EX	13	TA	9

Length	TB	79	TB	80	TB	81	TB	82	TB	83	TB	84	TA	10

Weight	TB	85	TB	86	TA	11

Volume/Capacity	TB	87	TB	88	TB	89	TB	90

Mixed measure	TB	91	TB	92

Area	TB	93	TB	94	TB	95	TB	96	TB	97	EX	19

Shape

2D Shape: line symmetry	TB	98

2D Shape: properties, puzzles and patterns	TB	99	TB	100	TB	101	TB	102	TB	103	TB	104	EX	14
	EX	15	EX	16	EX	17	EX	18	TA	13a	TA	13b		

3D Shape	TB	105	TB	106	TB	107	TB	108

Position, movement and angle	TB	109	TB	110	TB	111	TB	112	TA	14a	TA	14b

Data Handling

Interpreting graphs/data	TB	113	TB	114	TB	115	TB	116	TB	117	EX	20	EX	21

Bar charts with class intervals	TB	118	EX	22

Spreadsheets and databases	TB	119	TB	120	TB	121	TB	122

Language of probability	TB	123	TA	15